Communication in Corporate Climate

Communication in Corporate Climate

Dr. Urmi Satyan

Dr. Chaitanya Vyas

KALPAZ

First Published, 2021

Published by

Kalpaz Publications
C-30, Satyawati Nagar,
Delhi – 110052
Ph.: 011-47034999, 9811692060
www.kalpazpublications.com
E-mail: kalpaz@hotmail.com

Printed at: Gyan Press, Delhi.

Cataloging in Publication Data—DK
Courtesy: D.K. Agencies (P) Ltd. <docinfo@dkagencies.com>

Satyan, Urmi, author.
Communication in corporate climate / Dr. Urmi Satyan, Dr. Chaitanya Vyas.
pages cm
ISBN 9789353246259

1. Communication in management. 2. Business communication. I. Vyas, Chaitanya, 1981- author. II. Title.

LCC HD30.3.S28 2021 | DDC 658.45 23

Contents

Preface

It nurtures one's faith in creative talent to see the invisible labour behind it getting transformed into a tangible shape of a book and thus being able to contribute a little to the existing pool of knowledge. Some such faith is instated in us while offering the present book *Communication in Corporate Climate* to the world of knowledge. It is a proven fact that Corporate Communication is a mix of creative and critical thinking. It is strategic, diplomatic and formal. Communication in corporate world combines rich theoretical background with practical implications. In today's dynamic corporate climate, communication is more a criterion to be successful than only to be recognised as an essential tool or skill. With this point of view, we make a humble attempt to explore some of the intricacies of corporate communication. The book is designed and elaborated also to help the corporate personalities to effortlessly walk through the labyrinthine twists and turns of corporate world. With different but complimentary backgrounds of language and business, we authors have given our best to bring in together our perspectives, experiences and understandings in this book. We are sure that the book will capture attention of students, researchers and practicing corporate professionals.

The first chapter in the book elaborates corporate climate and communication practices. This chapter introduces topics like communication cycle, communication barriers, aspects of formal communication, and linguistic variations.

The second chapter highlights office politics and office personalities. The topics discussed here are competitive atmosphere and the required skillsets, negative and positive facets of office politics, multi-cultural milieu – the mosaic of corporate house, expected and choice-based behaviour, and barriers to effective communication.

The third chapter deals with strategic communication, a key to be successful corporate communicator.

The fourth chapter relates the nuances of advertising and communication. This chapter sees advertisement in the backdrop of culture, psychology, history, art/aesthetics, and education. It also explains formats and methods of advertisement, and features of advertisement.

The fifth chapter describes very important dimensions of communication i.e., art of negotiation. The chapter focuses on negotiation in personal and professional circles, the roadmap of negotiation, and some negotiation etiquettes.

The sixth chapter explains what crisis is, SWOT analysis of crisis, multifaceted role of linguistic precision, types of crisis, and committees or teams to manage crisis.

The seventh chapter in this book details four essential skills– Listening, Speaking, Reading, and Writing – as the infrastructural pillars of communication. Exercises are given at the end of each section.

The eighth chapter visits some popular theories and models in communication. Some communication models and theories are summarised both alphabetically and chronologically.

The last but not the least, **chapter nine** narrates selected classic fables that find relevance with today's corporate world. These fables give subtle morals and quintessential messages that are easy to be remembered and adopted at workplaces.

Though we faced many challenges while writing this book, we believe that we have overcome them all with patience, diligence and strong coordination. We are hopeful that the book will surely be a choice of the readers like aspiring students and researchers and also the practicing corporate officials.

Dr. Urmi Satyan
Dr. Chaitanya Vyas

Acknowledgement

During the unprecedented Covid – 19 Pandemic when frequent lockdowns and work from home orders were quite rampant as our safety measures, it was almost impossible to complete writing this present book; especially when one of us got tested Corona positive. If at all we have maintained the maddening stride and have achieved our mission without any big *jab*; we owe a big *thank you* to our spouses (Satyan Dave and Archa Vyas), our kids (Shreya & Shreyas and Saumyaa & Saanvi) and their incredible backing and love. Their strong support and patience have been the incessant driving force.

In addition, we are greatly indebted to the descent work culture and to the library, a rich reservoir of knowledge, both at School of Liberal Studies, Pandit Deendayal Energy University – our workplace.

Finally, we are grateful to the divine grace that we all experience in the form of humanity, honesty and loyalty.

Dr. Urmi Satyan
Dr. Chaitanya Vyas

List of Figures

Chapter - 1

Corporate Communication

Communication is the lifeline of human survival. To imagine a life without communication is like thinking about speech without sound. We communicate through language, expressions and postures.

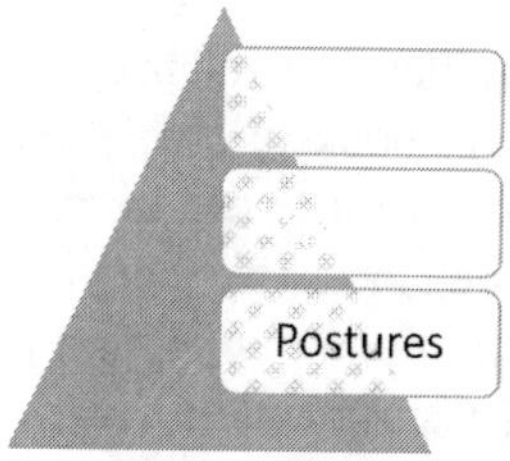

Source: Authors' representation.

Figure 1: Language, Expression and Postures.

In absence of these three modes of communication, human life will perish and extinct. Communication serves the basic four purposes of human life; the purpose of sharing, exchanging, acknowledging, and growing. These four purposes work in circular motion and they define the material, moral and also the metaphysical existence of human life. Thus, communication is a two-way process where the speaker is responsible to convey and the listener is responsible to comprehend. Comprehension helps the listener to provide feedback to the speaker. Basically,

Communication is a Cycle of 3 Cs: Convey to Comprehend to Convey. This cycle gets affected if any barrier obstructs its circular motion.

Source: Authors' representation.

Figure 2: Cycle of 3 Cs

Barriers to Communication

Communication is a circular motion as the speaker and the listener both end with conveying the meaning. The speaker conveys some concern, information or message and the listener, as a result of the comprehension, conveys back to the speaker that the concern, information or message is received. In case the listener fails to convey the comprehended message, there is noticed some barriers and the circular motion of communication gets affected. Mainly, there are four major types of barriers that can disrupt the process of communication. These barriers are:

1. **Linguistic Barrier**

   It is just impossible to have a meaningful communication where both the performers do not know each other's language. In such situations, expressions and postures – the other two modes of communication function as supportive modes. They cannot take lead roles in establishing meaningful communication. May the communication be formal or informal, the cycle of three Cs – convey-comprehend-convey ought to be completed for a meaningful communication. No communication is registered or documented when the speaker and the listener hail from different linguistic backgrounds. For effective communication, it is necessary to remove all the gaps from the meaningful communication. Every sentence in communication is meaningful, a complete whole, where word and meaning are strongly connected to each other. If any gap takes place between word and meaning, communication cycle gets disrupted. There are more chances for the message to be misinterpreted or misunderstood in case of disrupted communication.

2. Cultural Barrier

Culture frames the identity of human beings. Our culture gets reflected through our behaviour, mannerisms, language and accent, dressing style, religious faith, and belief system. The world today is a global village; the global market economy has paved the way for the beyond border connections. The rising globalisation has given birth to multiculturalism. Nevertheless, our ethnic culture is always protected and followed as a sign of our proud obligation to our mother culture. A corporate person may be a renowned global personality yet his/her ethnic culture is quite prominent in identity framing. Cultural differences can create barrier to effective communication. The cultural differences are noticed in the ways to greet the way Indians, Japanese and the English greet each other. Indians would say Namaste with folded hands, Japanese would bow down as a sign of greeting and the English would shake hand and make a cheek-to-cheek touch to greet. Indians may use hands to eat, English use spoons and Chinese use chop sticks. Such differences, sometimes, affect effective communication.

3. Temperamental Barrier

Humans and their temperaments are inseparable. A human being perceives, responds, reacts, thinks, behaves, works and contributes in tune with his/her temperament. Temperament can basically be divided into two categories. Exclusive and Inclusive. Let us study the characteristic features of these temperaments:

Exclusive Temperament: Employees with this temperament tend to avoid extra mingling and networking. They are more introvert and do not share their personal space with others. They are keen about their work responsibilities and take full ownership of their duties. These people are comfortable working alone and not in teams. They avoid leadership and followership both. In case they are forced to work against their temperament, they struggle first to arrange things in accordance with their temperament, apply selective approach in forming their teams and also design the roadmap that easily suits their 'exclusive' working pattern.

Inclusive Temperament: Adopt, adjust and associate – is the 3A formula for employees with inclusive temperament. They are not hesitant to adopt new technicalities or approaches. They easily get adjusted to the changing environment and they associate without any preconceived notion. They are friendly, approachable and welcoming. They encourage sharing and exchanging of ideas. They believe in group work. Their exceptional sociable qualities help them grow as team leaders. They have persuasive abilities and marketing skills. The open mindedness of these employees make them popular among colleagues. These people are sometimes found talkative and so also irksome and time consuming. Nevertheless, their friendliness keep the office ambience stress free.

Temperamental attitude is the reflection of the basic nature. An arrogant or self-surrounded person would be more exclusive and a friendly and approachable person would be more inclusive. Both attitudes have their advantages and disadvantages. Communication gets disrupted when the temperaments of the employees don't match. A corporate employee must remove the temperamental barrier to meet the requirement of his/her job profile.

4. **Subject-Knowledge Barrier**

   Today's nature of corporate work demands expertise over the subject-knowledge. May the type of work be assignments, projects, presentations, national/international meetings or analytical surveys of the production/ sales/manufacturing departments; all types of works are carried out under rigorous brain storming, planning and execution. It is necessary for the group members to be on the same page of subject-knowledge. If the group members hail from different backgrounds of knowledge, the task accomplishment would be under doubt. Critical and innovative ideas take place when the group members are competent to communicate their ideas over the subject-knowledge. A group with equal subject knowledge can:

   1. Enhance the learning skills
   2. Introduce innovative ideas
   3. Comprehend easily
   4. Contribute prolifically
   5. Manage the work-flow
   6. Proceed coherently

These advantages help the group to fight the challenges and address all the diverse issues that come their way. Such a group prepares the roadmap explicitly and works with extra attention to get the desired result. Subject knowledge barrier affects the coherent and collaborative approach to accomplish any task in the organisation. The figure given below is an attempt to easily explain the four barriers to effective communication.

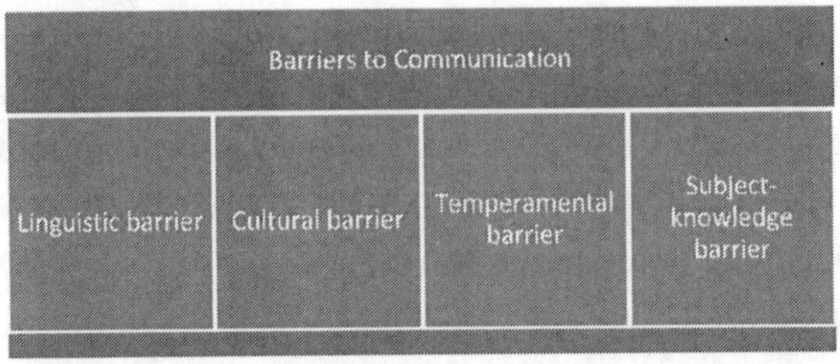

Source: Authors' representation.

Figure 3: Barriers to Communications.

Corporate communication is mostly formal in nature except in case of some personal familiarity and connection. Formal communication can be upward (bottom to top), downward (top to bottom) or lateral (among the colleagues with equal status and position). This communication takes place in the forms of written correspondence either through (a) Notice, (b) Memo, (c) e-mail, (d) requisition forms, (e) undertakings, (f) contracts and (g) the set of letters – Request letter, order letter, appraisal letter, recommendation letter, complaint letter, enquiry letter etc. The structure and layout of these formal communications should be strictly adhered. We have studied the basic structure of this formal correspondence modes at the undergraduate level. Here we will study the four essential aspects, as elaborated below, of the formal communication.

Four Essential Aspects of Formal Communication

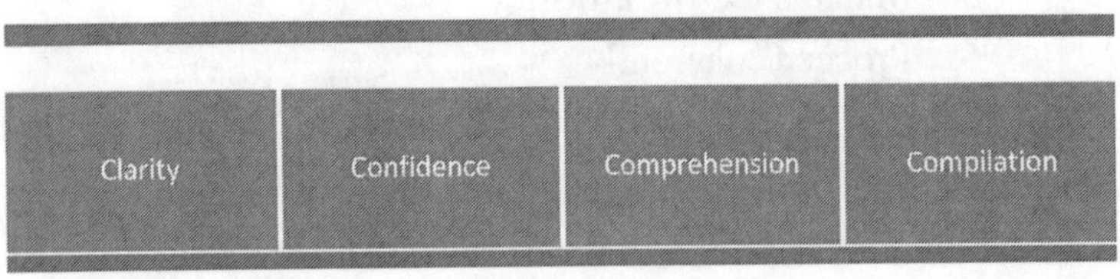

Source: Authors' representation.

Figure 4: Four Essential Aspects of Formal Communication.

Clarity

Communication has a circular cycle of 3Cs as studied in the

beginning of this chapter. Therefore, it is necessary that the group in communication is well informed about the point/s of discussion. Any ambiguous message or convoluted instruction can badly affect communication. For example, before calling a meeting, a CEO must set an agenda that clearly specifies whether it is a Review Meeting, Decision Making, Policy Making or Problem Solving Meeting. A Review Meeting is generally about performance appraisal. Such meetings encourage the employee to contribute more efficiently to the organisation. These meetings are arranged also to brainstorm on a particular issue, to prepare an organogram, to provide accurate feedback, to explain the roadmap for the upcoming activities and sometimes also to build trust and strengthen the professional relationship among employees. Thus, clarity is the key to successfully achieve the target. Clarity is synonymous with transparency that easily controls politics, conflicts or any discrepancy.

Confidence

Confidence results from factual correctness. A well informed/ researched employee speaks with confidence. Such a person never undertakes any assignment casually and so prefers to remain updated about the activities in their surroundings. This makes their communication more relevant and contextual. To be a confident speaker one must build connections with inter-organisational groups and thus widen the chances for more and more intellectual exchanges of ideas. A confident person can also become an influential public speaker. To speak with confidence is an art that easily attracts and influences people. To develop this art to speak with confidence, one needs to take care of the matter and manner. A confident person stands upright with professional attire and posture. A confident speaker easily sets the ball rolling and gets the message circulated quickly and impressively. Confidence is also necessary for the personal and career growth. When a speaker lacks confidence, nervousness overpowers, as a result of which one may forget the important points from the discussion and consequently lose the attention of the listeners. It is an essential skill that one may learn to discover the hidden talent of abilities. This skill instils belief in oneself. The use of the words like 'definitely', 'certainly', 'why not', 'of course', 'sure' etc., further enhances the power of self-confidence. A confident person speaks fluently and proficiently. On one side they flawlessly quote renowned authors and on other they mention facts and figures with aplomb. They logically arrange their arguments and use the persuasive power to win the attention of the listeners. Such speakers avoid self-effacing sentences like 'I don't know', 'I have a fear of…' 'I don't understand' etc. In case they want to make any confessional statement, they will not sound negative about their abilities but they will show the valour to turn the story of struggle into the story of success. A confident person can win half the battle in the corporate world.

Comprehension

Comprehension is imperative for successful communication. The act of comprehension is silent and internal. The microscopic view of comprehension can be understood with the help of the Comprehension Flowchart as stated in Figure 5.

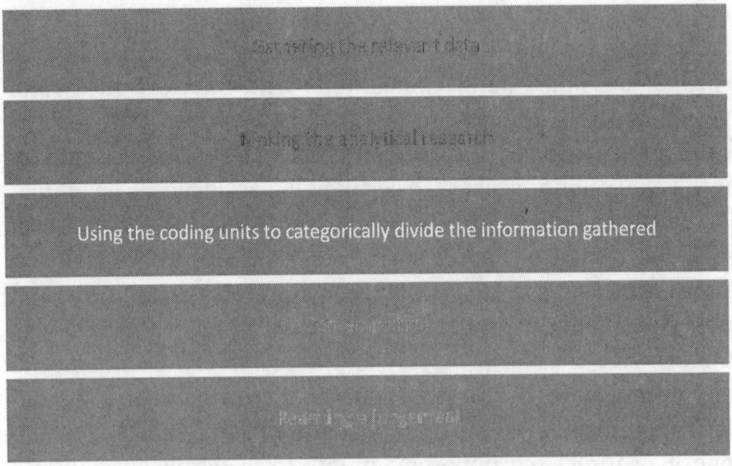

Source: Authors' representation.

Figure 5: **Comprehension Flowchart.**

Communication in the professional world is always planned and organised. This type of communication is purposeful and time bound. The employees associated in such communication must comprehend the conceptual and contextual message from the communication. Unless the message is comprehended by all, any communication does not reach the stage of completion. Accurate comprehension also leads the communication to satisfaction that further complements and supports the three most valuable key features of corporate communication –innovative thinking, strategic planning and decision making. Thinking includes the past references and future relevance of the study, planning includes brainstorming and decision-making includes the conclusion of the communication with the remarks followed by the action plans. Comprehension also includes imagination and logical reasoning.

Compilation

Compiling minutes, agenda, work flow, day to day reporting, review reports and also further roadmaps; all information and activity-flows should be maintained for future references. Proper labelling with subject and date saves time and energy while referring to them in future. There should also be year wise compilation. The habit of compilation also teaches tidiness, accuracy and discipline. A sincere and dedicated employee in a corporate world shoulders many responsibilities. The communication flow changes from one to the other matters. If the progress of every matter is not filed properly, further proceedings get affected. Any diligent employee would surely spare some time in compiling the everyday progress of/in thc matter/s under discussion to avoid waste of time and energy. Now, the compilation task is almost digitalised. The task of compilation has become easier. Nevertheless, one needs to take care in saving the files with proper names for a smooth function in future. Compilation also helps us analyse the chain of work as well as the decisions taken by the company in the past. Compilation followed by the analytical study helps identify the shortcomings in the workflow and further methodise the action plan for better resolution. Compilation is all about data management. Reference to the properly managed data adds a touch of clarity, confidence and thus widens the scope for future operational tasks. Corporate world is non-ending, however compilation can be interpreted as the full and complete form of communication for a particular matter on hand.

The barrier-free environment and the qualities of clarity, confidence, comprehension and compilation can transform a casual conversation into the concrete communication – a key to the well managed and constructive corporate life. These qualities benefit a leader as well as an employee. In lack of these qualities, an employee may appear inadequate and clumsy. These qualities enhance the work culture and pave the way for optimum utilisation of knowledge and experience gained from the past. Corporate communication functions at various levels – upward, downward, horizontal and also local, national and/or international levels. Corporate communication is not only between two parties or employees, it can be between two or more companies/nations. A smallest disruption in communication chain can affect the effectiveness of it. Resultantly, it can also affect the image and reputation of the company. Corporate communication has to be well-planned and strategic to operate most effectively.

Corporate Communication with Difference

When the French philosopher Jacques Derrida crafted the word "differAnce" by deconstructing the dictionary word 'difference' and introducing a novel approach to the same, he intended to draw our attention to the difference that we discern from any word at connotative and denotative levels. He also intended to exhibit that replacing 'e' with 'a' in the spelling, does not affect the pronunciation and meaning of the words. Yet, the intention is to highlight the difference, for sure. Corporate communication demands 'difference' that brings impressiveness. Difference shows speaker's efforts to present the matter effectively, emphatically and expressively. Difference is added when the speaker uses the ability to express meaningfully. A meaningful and effective communication needs the ability to sort and filter from plethora of ideas that are relevant, prioritised and arranged effectively. This difference can be noticed at the contextual level that helps decode the intention associated with the matter of discussion.

It is very interesting to note that intention is associated with context. In one of his poems named

Turning and turning in the widening gyre
The falcon cannot hear the falconer;

Yeats brings to our attention an image of a falcon (a bird) who is departed from its falconer (the handler) and is turning and turning in the widening gyre (spiral like funnel of smoke). The contextual meaning associates the falcon to the human soul and the falconer to the supreme one. A teacher or a parent may also interpret the falcon to be a student/child and themselves as the falconer. (The poem has biblical reference).

Intention can also be deciphered through the tone of a speaker. When Caesar says, "You too Brutus!" it reveals his deep shock. For Caesar, the pain of being killed is less than the pain of being deceived. It is only through the tone that Caesar expresses his pain over betrayal and treachery by a close person. This three word sentence with one as a proper noun (Brutus) has almost become an expression of the pinnacle of betrayal. Until the reader pans out the contextual meaning, the reading remains hazy, vague and inconclusive. Thus, the intention is revealed when reading is done comprehensively. Now comes a pertinent question, How to read comprehensively? Words and their respective meanings are inseparable and the reader dexterously unearths the associated meaning.

In a corporate world, intentions are presented through four linguistic expressions like:

1. Language of Confidence
2. Language of Appraisal

3. Language of Assertion
4. Language of Humour

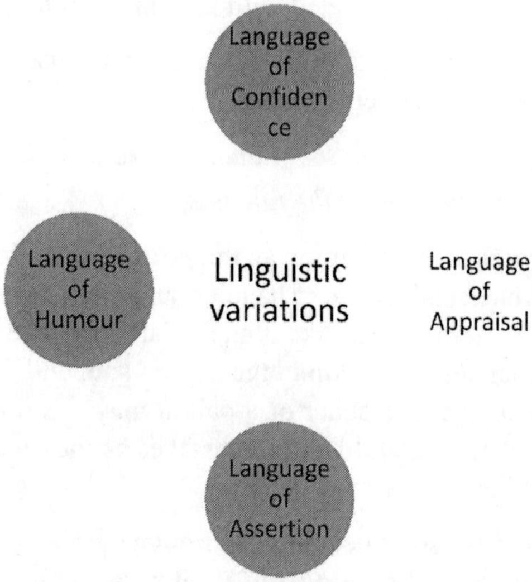

Source: Authors' representation.

Figure 6. Four Linguistic Expressions.

Language of Confidence

A confident speaker wins half the battle. Any prospective employee should remember that the first impression is, mostly, the last impression. One more dictum is also popular that opportunity knocks the door only once. There can't be any replacement of the language of confidence. Confidence has four pillars:

1. Subject Knowledge
2. Linguistic Power
3. Body Language
4. Accessories

1. **Subject Knowledge:** We are living in the information-packed time where we all are flooded with information. The credit for this must be given to the incessant telecast

of new channels on television and social media platforms. We come across information from everywhere and so we remain well-informed about the events taking place around us. Subject knowledge is different to information. Subject knowledge is a subject completely, thoroughly. Subject knowledge ranges from eavesdropped information to conceptualised matter. In short, when an information is tested, explored and conceptualised, it takes the form of knowledge. Such subject knowledge brings confidence and there is no short-cut to gain confidence and be knowledgeable. It is nothing but the result of the hard work. Also, the self-acquired subject knowledge is irreplaceable, un-exchangeable and un-alterable. Such hard earned subject knowledge instils confidence to the brim which gets reflected when a person speaks.

2. **Linguistic Power:** Language introduces a person's knowledge, ability and thinking pattern. Language is a mirror of a person's personality. Linguistic power is attained by a strong association with the linguistic ornaments like rich vocabulary, idiomatic usages, phrasal verbs, figures of speech and umpteen number of proverbial statements. English is an official language in India but it is the second language. So English language speakers need to acquire it thoroughly.
3. **Body Language:** People think body language is natural and it can't be worked upon. But we need to remember that body language is the most powerful non-verbal communication feature. A very succinct example can be taken from the Indian dance forms like Bharatnatyam, Kathak, Kuchipudi, Kathakali and many more where the performer speaks only through body language. Some dos and don'ts maybe summarised thus:

Dos for body language:

1. Stand upright. See that you are not bent from your west and neck.

2. Make proper eye-contact.
3. Maintain at least 1/5 to 2 feet distance from the listener.
4. Make a firm hand-shake.
5. Stand up to greet in the formal setting.
6. Maintain the audible pitch of your voice.
7. Remain well dressed, from head to toe.
8. Keep hands free or folded and position them with natural straightness.
9. While listening, be expressive by using mono-syllabic words like 'hmm' , 'oh'. This is to make the speaker feel that you are attentive.
10. By the end of the conversation, share the visiting card and a verbal note of pleasure meeting.

Don'ts

1. Don't lean towards the speaker if you are the listener.
2. Don't look here and there, at the background or on the things lying on the table.
3. Don't be very far or very close to the speaker.
4. Hand shake is just a greeting gesture. Hand shake should not continue for more than 10-15 seconds.
5. Don't greet while being seated on the chair.
6. Don't be louder or lower with your pitch of voice.
7. Formal dressing should not be compromised with.
8. Don't put your hands in the pocket or hold a piece of cloth in your hand.
9. Just use expressive sounds while listening. Don't cut the speaker to convey your knowledge over the matter.
10. Don't offer the visiting card with one hand. Offer holding it with both the hands. It is respect of the card (your hard earned position) as well as the other.

Though body language is the non-verbal way to communicate and so mostly it is understood as natural and inherited. Yet, a good observatory skills may bring to our notice how body language enhances the speaker's presentability.

Accessories

We all are living in the technological world. Our businesses today are digitalised. The banking system, the legal system, many of the public sectors, income tax sector – almost every sector of human life is digitalised. In fact, we are living in a digital world. According to a Gujarati proverb, "A poet reaches where the Sun can't reach". It means, a poet's power of imagination is richer than the power of the Sunrays. In case we want to attach a rejoinder to the proverb we can say, "Technology reaches where even a poet can't reach". Though it is just a way to explain the power of technology. Accessories are necessities and not luxuries in the present life. The list of accessories include:

1. **Electronic gazettes:** The electronic gazettes like laptop, mobile phone, printer etc. help us store multiple files and documents. It is unnecessary to write here that these gazettes are the best if used wisely, judiciously and meticulously. Here, the attention is drawn towards utilising the e-equipments for one or the other creative purpose and not only to binge watching and mindless surfing.
2. **Required Stationary:** In addition to these gazettes, the basic stationary like an executive diary, a ball pen and a pencil surely helps to enhance the aesthetic look and also to note down the important points immediately. Also, one can refer to the diary for better management with everyday commitments and priorities. However, a smart mobile phone is not less than a diary.
3. **Personality enhancers:** These are the accessories that work as the cherry on the cake. One can eat an undecorated cake but to have it, is idyllic. Cherry enhances the beauty as well as the flavour of the cake. Similarly, an ironed

handkerchief (in case needs to be used in a formal meeting), good cufflinks, tie or bow, polished shoes, proper hairstyle and a touch of good perfume certainly enhances personality. We should be careful that these accessories should be used in minimum numbers, nothing should look like a pomp and show.

Having said this, it is imperative to bring to the surface that "Knowledge is irreplaceable". Only accessories can't make a person impressive if he/she is devoid of knowledge.

Language of Praise

Praise brings a childlike smile on the receiver's face. To praise is to acknowledge, to make the person feel that the services rendered by him/her are well recorded and have not gone in vain. Praise works as a verbal reward. In the corporate world, praise is a kind of incentive, motivation and encouragement. In a corporate culture, praise has a downward communication flow. The employer acknowledges the employee's services. Such acknowledgement has a double effect – it motivates the person in subject for more dedication and commitment as well as it inspires other employees to grow more and be the assets and not the liabilities for the company. The words of praise may be showered on the employee in these manners:

1. A celebration party maybe arranged for some unique achievement of the employee.
2. The family of the concerned maybe invited to the party.
3. The concerned may be given a well framed Letter of Appreciation.
4. The concerned may also be offered a sponsored mini vacation with family.
5. Some monetary incentives or promotion in the position certainly inspires.

Such words of appreciation creates positive environment that further works as a force and helps establish harmonious environment. This kind of openness completely evades any matter of differences, biases, inequalities and discriminations. The employer should never hesitate or delay in acknowledging any service received from the employee. This is to avoid any doubt and suspicion taking birth in the horizontal line of the employees.

Language of Assertion

Life is full of challenges, changes and chains. Many times, one needs to face the challenge, accept the changes and also break the chains. The British dramatist Bernard Shaw rightly says, "Progress is impossible without change and those who cannot change their minds cannot change anything". A person who introduces change becomes a trend setter and that affect the society at large. This is simply an emergence of identity. There comes time when one puts the foot down and gets assertive. This is necessary for a leader as well as the followers. To be assertive means to be courageous. There comes time when one realises, "If not now, never". The language of assertion is the language of clarity. To be assertive is not to be understood as to be aggressive. One can be soft and express his/her assertion. Language of assertion is the language of courage that puts one under the highlight or the spotlight. A clear mind signifies specificity, punctuality and reliability. A clear mind takes the worry off the table, it keeps any kind of unpleasant incident at bay.

Assertion also helps person to be more focused and deterministic. Assertion can be presented by being soft. Assertion vouches for one's self-esteem and self-confidence. An assertive person appears focused and direct. The most interesting thing about assertion is that it demands others also to be the same. A puzzled, baffled or convoluted person would not be able to present him/herself properly in front of an assertive person. An assertive person has a higher chance to be recognized by the senior management. An assertive person remains the same also during the time of loss. He/she courageously accepts if there is any fault on their side. They can't accept any unethical mean for a speedy rise and that brings reverence for them at a workplace.

However, such a person must ably distinguish assertion to aggression as there is a thin line of distinction between the two. Aggression is a state of anger that washes out all the positive energy of the person. As assertion is a strength, aggression is weakness. One must remember that a workplace demands exhibition of the power of the mind and not the power of the body.

Language of Humour

A touch of humour makes one approachable, accessible and amiable. It is an essential skill to communicate and thus to socialise. It relieve the person who holds it and also them with whom it is shared. Humour is actually a weapon to remove stress at workplace. It helps one unmask the hidden child behind the formal appearance. Humour works as a *calm-er, cool-er.* A sense of humour provides immunity to the mental health. As it relieves the mind of the unprecedented tension, it helps bring glow on the skin. Medical science says, "Laughter is the best medicine". A humorous person would always carry smile on his/her face. Smile is in itself a sign of welcome, natural greeting, relief and open-mindedness. A humour-less person turns out to be a boring one. It becomes difficult for others to come and talk to such a boring person. The quality of humour is inevitable for a leader. When a leader talks humorously, the message of equality and nobility is conveyed.

Humour is also a sign of brilliance that includes sharp memory, knowledge over the national and international current affairs and the ability to build connection between some past event and the present. Humour is a sign of present wit and ready smartness. Humour is mostly a natural feature. However, a person can acquire this ability by observing others being prompt in citing the appropriate examples with the incident in the moment. This soft skill works powerfully. Humour wipes out any possibility of hate or conflict. This weapon can transform hatred and conflict into a harmonious and cordial relation. A leader with humorous nature instils enthusiasm to the employees, encourages them to be exclusive with their commitment towards workplace. Such a leader works like a peacemaker in the time of critical situation.

A humorous leader might use a story from history or mythology and connect the past with the present and thus establish a code of harmony and geniality.

These types of languages are associated with the speaker's emotions and so also with the body language. A speaker's expression speaks for his/her mind. Nevertheless, some words, phrases and idioms also make these linguistic variations more clearly presentable. Let us see some obvious words for each in the following table:

Language of Confidence	***Language of Appraisal***	***Language of Assertion***	***Language of Humour***
Sure	Good going	My strong suggestion is ...	Change the pronunciation and create humour as
Why not?	Energetic presentation	I will take my share by hook or crook	Your presentation was *to the point*. It was not at all a *storm in a teacup*. (Hullabaloo)
Very true	Your hard work is visible	I will never sigh a low deal	Please don't stretch your presentation for *donkey's years*. (extra time)
I second that opinion	You are always self-motivated	I can not tolerate unjust behaviour	I can answer all your questions but be sure that you will not pick my brain.
Without fail	You are honest to your emotions	I take the ownership of my statements	Your presentation was best since sliced bread (since 1928, the year when not the loaf but the slices of bread came to market in packets)
I am cock sure about that	Your perseverance will take you higher		At the time of good presentation, the boss says "it was entirely –untiring".
perfect	You are an asset to our corporate house		You need to score outstanding remarks otherwise you will stand out of the office.

Language: the Code of Intention

Language is the code of intention, purpose and objective. Intention is inter woven in a word – the smallest unit in a sentence that bears more of a pragmatic than semantic value.

Semantics

Semantics is one of the important branches of linguistics that deals with the meaning of words, sentence-structures and symbols. The meaning of the word is determined also on the reading comprehension of the readers, how the readers understand the word and its associated interpretations. William Frawley defines linguistic semantics as "the study of literal, decontextualised, grammatical meaning".[1] He gives three analytical observations:

1. "meanings that are actually reflected in overt form differences"
2. "what state of affairs…in the world [an] expression represents"
3. It "suggests about the speaker's intention"
4. the "meaning that is determinable outside of context" and
5. "meaning that is bound up with the mechanisms that language has for grammatical expression".

Thus, Semantics and pragmatics are branches of linguistics. Both of them deal with the study of meaning. Semantics deals with the study of meaning of word without the context. On the other hand, pragmatics understands meaning by keeping the context in mind. Semantics is concerned with the conceptual meaning related to words. Semantics does not focus on the context, rather it deals with the meaning according to grammar and vocabulary. The focus is only on the general rules used for a language. The study of linguistics is majorly divided into phonetics (speech sound), phonology (phonemes), morphology (words), syntax (phrases and sentences), semantics (literal meaning of phrases and sentences) and pragmatics. **Semantics** can be understood at two levels, Connotative and Denotative. **Connotative semantics** is the meaning that is associated with the word emotionally, imaginatively and metaphorically. The meaning is inferred by readers who can relate to the suggestions associated with the word. Simply, the reader takes the figurative meaning associated with the word. Usually poets use this type of meaning in their poetry.

Contrary to this, **Denotative Semantics** suggests the literal, explicit or dictionary meaning of the words without using associated meanings. It also uses symbols in writing that suggest expressions of writers such as an exclamation, quotation and colon marks.

Every word has a singular and stand-alone denotative meaning. It is the smallest unit in a sentence that represents an idea, object, action or place. Words can have more than one meaning. It is the characteristic of a word that it may have several meanings, in fact, words play an enormous part in panning out the meaning. Words express, convey and describe. Despite these features, words can not give a comprehensive meaning that is complete in itself. To get the cognitive meaning of the word, it needs to have a relation with the other parts of a sentence. A word is interpreted in relation to the experience, situation and time conveyed by other parts of the sentence.

Pragmatics

Pragmatics refers to the strategies, exploitation of shared knowledge, assumptions about communicative intent, by which language users relate the dictionary/grammar meaning of utterances to their communicative value in context. Pragmatics generally refers to the encoding of particular communicative functions, especially those relevant to interpersonal exchanges, in specific grammatical and lexical elements of a given language.

Pragmatics includes a wide range of topics and elements that help verifying the working process of all its elements which are listed below. While defining pragmatics, it is necessary that the listener is strong in perceiving, assuming, imagining and deducing the hidden meaning from the written text. **Entailment, Presupposition and Implicature** are the linguistic varieties that help discern the correct meaning from the given sentence.

Entailment is a relationship between two sentences where the truth of one requires the truth of the other. For example,

I will introduce you to my cousin in his birthday party.

The sentence entails that the speaker will invite the listener to the former's birthday party or the speaker knows that the listener is also invited to the party.

Presupposition is an utterance that is based on a background belief or prior knowledge. There can be a general assumption employed to reach an inference. It can present an assertion, denial, or question, and can be associated with a specific lexical item or grammatical feature in the utterance.

Eg: I could complete the task before office time.

It is presumed that he must be having a team of adequate employees.

Implicature is to read the implied meaning which is interwoven in the sentence but not meant to be conveyed. It is a technical term in the linguistic branch of pragmatics coined by Paul Grice who has introduced four Maxims – Quantity, Relation, Quality and Manner – that help infer the communicative intention and "inform our cooperative behaviour in general as guiding principles in inference drawing…that communicative intention is a pragmatic inference, based on what was said explicitly and contextual assumptions the speaker intends the addressee to consider in the computation of the inference". (Ariel: 2008; 9) Simply put, there are two meanings within a sentence. For example, "… And they lived happily ever after". Here, under the common presumptions, 'they' stands for a couple who fought against all odds and have successfully settled down and lived a happy married life.

Thus, the study of language is based mainly on three aspects, grammar, structure and meaning. The first two are present in the semantic and pragmatic understanding of the language. But the third aspect 'meaning' is more about the expressional interpretation than the verbal interpretation of language. The study of proverbs affirmatively substantiates this argument. Proverbs are the mirrors that reflect the society, culture and polity of a region.

In his paper Pragmatics, Robert Stalnaker writes,

> Syntax studies sentences, semantics studies propositions. Pragmatics is the study of linguistic acts and the contexts in which they are performed. There are two major types of problems to be solved within pragmatics: first, to define interesting types of speech acts and speech products; second, to characterise the features of the speech context which help determine which proposition is expressed by a given sentence.…Assertions, commands, counterfactuals, claims, conjectures and refutations, requests, rebuttals, predictions, promises, pleas, speculations, explanations, insults, inferences, guesses, generalisations, answers and lies are all kinds of linguistic acts. The problem of analysis in each case is to find necessary and sufficient conditions for the successful (or in some cases normal) performance of the act.[2]

Later in the essay, Stalnaker also discusses about **Pragmatic ambiguity.** He says, when there is a problem in determining the context and/or when there are possibilities of more than one contextual references; and also when a particular truth is not established, there arises a pragmatic ambiguity. The reader is stuck somewhere in the middle of the multiple possible interpretations and is forced to determine the contextual reference embedded in linguistic variations. In such situations, misconceptions and misunderstandings are more possible. To remove such linguistic ambiguities, comprehensive reading and listening (as discussed in this chapter) is the only solution.

Notes

1. Frawley, William, Kenneth C Litkowski. Review of Linguistic Semantics by William Frawley https://www.clres.com/online-papers/dsna94.html# Palmer
2. Robert Stalnaker “Pragmatics” Syntheses Vol. 22 No. 1/ 2 Semantics of Natural Language, II *https://www.jstor.org › stable*

Chapter - 2

Office Politics and Office Personalities

What is Office Politics?

Office politics is a survival strategy in a competitive world; it is a kind of natural reality that is intangible yet omnipresent, awkward yet exciting, influential yet unaffected and stubborn yet cooperative. These sets of oxymora show negative as well as positive aspects of office politics. It is basically a matter of perspective; a matter of mental strength and a matter of self-designed immunity booster. An office is a place for collective as well as individual vision and mission. An office comprises of a heterogeneous group of multi-talented employees who set their career goals and make all the possible efforts to achieve success. This aspiring cohort of employees dream to climb the ladder of success. Their dreams are fulfilled when the employees get fully acquainted with the challenges associated with workplace.

These challenges are divided into two parts, collective and individual. Collective challenges include responsibilities like working according to the vision and mission of the company and protecting the brand name of the company. Individual challenges are like creating rapport on the horizontal and vertical lines of colleagues, creating remarkable professional profile and also maintaining balance between professional and personal lives. Success in the professional life is possible if an employee understands these challenges, acts in accordance with the demand of the workplace and remains controlled, composed and consistent in pursuing his dreams.

The word "politics" draws our attention to something that must be controversial in nature, something that might provoke heated arguments, something that forces one towards competitive world, something that instigates the dormant feelings of anger, anxiety and agitation, something that does not boost one's moral encouragement and something that affects one's psychological as well as spiritual health. When these associated connotations start becoming the reality of one's life, the spiral of negative feeling can possibly envelop one and may force the same towards frustration and depression.

If only one changes the perception towards the word "politics"; one feels that it is something that can open a gateway of success. The word "power" is strongly associated with the word "politics". One who handles the politics well can easily become powerful and a powerful person can be a powerful contributor in the society. Here, the million dollar question is to know "how to handle politics?" Let us try to answer this question.

You all would agree that one can not participate half prepared in any debate that is related to either politics or religion. Politics and Religion are sensitive issues. If one does not have complete authority over these subjects, there are high chances of controversies, allegations and judgements. Similarly, to handle office politics, one needs to be well versed with it. There cannot be any toolkit that can be prescribed to an employee who can use it and get success in the professional life.

Office politics is a matter of experience without evidence and execution without event. And that is why mostly the term creates feelings of fear, insecurity and dissatisfaction. It does not have tangible aspects yet its powerful hold cannot be ignored. And that is why we can say that it is not curable but it is certainly controllable and *handleable*. And the tools to handle and control it are unique, subjective and reflective. We can't deny the fact that an office is a place of competitors, every employee is chasing a goalsheet – one given by the company and the other set by themselves. An office is a place where every employee keeps an eye on the grade points and also some brownie points. Such a competitive atmosphere demands a skill set from the employee. This skill-set comprises of some characteristics like:

Know Your Colleague

For a healthy competition, an employee must be aware of the strength of the colleague. This knowledge would surely enhance one's awareness about the prevalent competitiveness. One should not take somebody's strength as a threat but as a source of motivation to grow more in the organisation. This is how one can easily stop the negative influx of jealousy or insecurity and one can transfer the same into an opportunity to set a higher bar for personal success. Eventually, such an employee turns out to be a noticeable contributor in the growth of the organisation.

Improve Interpersonal Skills

In the present day, an office is a place of multi-cultural workers. On a linear scale all may be equal but their food-habits, belief-systems and feasts and festivals may vary as all belong to different cultures. Such differences should be considered as the colours in a rainbow. The cultural or linguistic barriers should be ignored and one must make all the honest efforts to bridge over the gaps. Such efforts pay off well by boosting self-morale and creating warm ambience and thus allowing positivity to be settled. This will also help building good connections with colleagues. Interpersonal skills are also about active listening and active participation in all the positive affairs. It is about respecting the opinions of others and also presenting our opinions, suggestions and thoughts among colleagues. Interpersonal skills make one accessible, approachable and amiable.

Be Clear and Focused

Clarity about oneself, one's goals and abilities and focus over the target leads an energetic employee to grow fast and steady.

One does not need to be loud and vocal about the same but focus and clarity would surely keep one grounded. These characteristics also bring repute. A clear and focused person would never agree to compromise with the value ethics. However, the path to success becomes a little longer but it surely takes one to the destination. Clarity also saves time and energy from any involvement into unnecessary and unimportant chatter or gossip. There are very low chances to get diverted and eventually lost if an employee has clarity over the productive and creative engagement in the office.

Strike a Balance between Professional and Personal Aims

An overburdened employee would bring the work and worries home which will disrupt personal life. One must remember that an overburdened employee is thc one who is not organised and meticulous about time. We all live in a digital world so keeping a personal diary or creating a planner or setting reminders are not difficult tasks. If one can follow the timeline strictly, there would be no spill over of the professional work over the personal one. Scheduling is a right technic to reduce unnecessary wanderings and hastings and also managing both the fronts of life.

There are many such skill-sets that help one to grow and be more productive. Before developing or applying these skillsets, one needs to understand the positive and negative aspects of office politics. This knowledge helps one recognise the causes and effects of Office Politics and also suggests some remedies to handle Office Politics with dexterity. In the light of this understanding, it would not be wrong to say that office politics is a Mind Game, a game like Chess where one's weakness is other's strength; one's poor performance opens a wider gate for other to perform well and get recognition. Studying the following ten features of negative and positive aspects of office politics will help develop the observatory and analytical skills and to act as per the requirement and be more competently and contributively immersive. Let us study these aspects in pairs to get an overall impact of the same.

Negative and Positive Aspects of Office Politics

A Negative Aspects of Office Politics	B Positive Aspects of Office Politics
1. Demanding	1. Contributing
2. Stressful	2. Engaging
3. Challenging	3. Benefitting
4. Dull	4. Dynamic
5. Demotivating	5. Negotiating
6. Compromising	6. Corresponding
7. Followership	7. Leadership
8. Conflicting	8. cooperative
9. Complaining	9. complementing
10. Separating	10. Mobilising

Demanding Vs. Contributing

Office demands dedication, determination and diligence. We see it often that employees misinterpret these demands as drudgery. Some think that office makes them work more than needed and some feel that they are forced to work in free as they do not see any immediate and noticeable rise in their salary. Such employees normally work for their short term goals. They overlook the learning that they get out of the work. One should remember that proverb that says, "Rome cannot be built in a day". If employees can perceive the demands of the office as a chance to be an active performer and contributor; he/she can definitely change the unfavourable aspects into favourable ones. A young and budding employee can contribute by taking up new challenges, walking an extra mile and catering to the expectations of the office. Such efforts never remain unrecognised or unacknowledged by the organisation. Sooner or later, such an employee get what they deserve to. A middle age employee can use his/her network to bring consultancies and projects for a company. His/her experience-sharing can also help fulfil the demands of an organisation. A Veteran employee may be an advisor and guide to others. The employees need to understand that the demands of an office are not exploitative but are providing opportunities to learn, grow and be active contributors.

Stressful Vs Engaging

An employee needs to decide whether he/she wants to carry a mundane or a remarkable life. An employee experiences stress when things are not as per the expected comfort and convenience; when his aspirations clash with that of the company's and when he considers the duties as burdens. A positive employee would convert stress into a chance to be engaged in active participation. When an employee feels overburdened, he/she experiences stress that kills creativity, mentally disturbs and also provokes thoughts of leaving the job. Once such ideas strike, it becomes difficult for the employee to work and grow. Stress can be handled by merely changing the perspective. When one feels overburdened, all the negative feelings of injustice and discriminations surround and the employee unknowingly ends up being negative and unproductive. Such employees need to make conscious efforts to consider it as an opportunity to be creatively engaged and be an active performer in the profit of the organisation. One must remember that any extra work done for the organisation is an investment and not divestment.

In addition, one must remember that one works for the benefit of the organisation and not for any person. This thought will protect honesty, boost morale and relieve him/her from any stressful distraction.

Challenging Vs Profiting

A threat can inflict pain, can damage one's work capacity and distracts focus and derails the work system. Threat is experienced in the times of job insecurity, cultural isolation, linguistic barrier or selective approach of the head of the organisation. Threat needs to be handled with intelligence. One must know that an organisation can grow only on the basis of work. A person who works with persistence and diligence gets recognised sooner or later. With such intelligent steps, threats can be transformed as challenges. When some tasks are taken as challenges, one starts feeling strong. A challenge motivates one to discover the hidden ability and potential. One invokes the inner strength that provides him/her a scope to prepare a roadmap to deal with the tangled web of complexities. To convert threat into a positive challenge, one must prepare a departmental plan for the easy and hassle-free function of office. As it is rightly claimed in a proverbial statement, "Where there is a will there is a way", any threat can be easily converted into a positive challenge. It is a matter of mind-set.

Dull Vs Dynamic

The world has become a global village. It would not be wrong to say that the digital technology has removed distances. This is the time when a simple conference call can connect corporate houses from different corners of the world. This diversity is necessary for an organisation to grow on international platform. Those who complain for this diverse nature of the work are bound to find themselves surrounded by the negative emotions. They appear dull in front of their colleagues and thus feel misfitting in the organisation. Contrary to this, if one can accept the work system, one can transform oneself from a dull to a dynamic personality. It is majorly a responsibility of the leader/head in the office to take understand the aspects associated with dynamism. The leader should pay more attention to the overall productivity of an employee than keeping an account of the hours spent in the office premises. Unreasonable force can make the office culture dull and down.

Demotivating Vs Negotiating

Motivation is derived from praises and praises are generated out of success-stories. Success-stories are created after hard work and hard work is the result of firm determination. Thus, well-founded determination is the key to feel motivated. If an employee lacks determination to reach out to the pinnacle of success, he/she surely ends up being demotivated. Demotivation can be addressed by being intellectually self-negotiating. An employee spends at least 7-8 hours a day at the work place. Self-negotiation forces one to weigh the profit and loss that he/she incurs out of the active/passive participation in the organisation. One can also feel motivated to observe others managing with the work responsibilities. Some negotiations with lethargy and contemplation over the consequences of the same leads one towards the path of intellectual occupancy.

Compromising Vs Corresponding

The employees who do not feel motivated, who feel over-burdened or misfit in the organisation, sometime end up subscribing to a compromise with the situation. The habit of compromising is not good for the employee's personal as well as professional growth. This habit becomes nature in no times. Compromising nature leads one towards a quick success and also an abrupt fall. Such a person loses moral courage. It is a kind of sugar coated poison that gives a short term success but in the long run damages an employee's reputation. He/she feels embarrassed when confronted with the hard working colleagues and thus they end up adding nothing but insult to injury. Contrary to this is a corresponding nature where an employee agrees with the terms and conditions and works in favour of the organisation. An ethical person may face some difficulties and may find that the path of ethical compromise is easy and close to the destination but when experienced, it is altogether a different result. As we all know that success can never have a short cut.

Followership Vs Leadership

Some employees feel that to follow the rules is like being submissive. Some feel that to follow is to obey the orders of the seniors and to accept the secondary status. Such employees overlook the learning that they get out of their followership. A follower is in a way an intern, an apprentice who learns more than what is earned. Such employees must understand that every ounce of service is not to be weighed in terms of money. The value of work experience should not be compared only with the monetary benefits. Also, personal grudge, prejudice or complex are the biggest hindrances that block the path of knowledge as well as success. If a follower thinks that the leader has a comfortable life, he just orders and observes; the former is utterly wrong. In a corporate world, no job, no position is sans the amount of worries and labour. Those who diligently handle such stressful emotions, find the path easy. It is not wrong to say that a good follower actually develops the qualities of a good leader.

Conflicting Vs Cooperative

There can not be any place – home or office; any relation – personal or professional or any matter – local or global where conflict does not exist. Every mind is a world and every world is unique. Everyone has to survive in this cut throat competitive world where pursuit of power is more focused than pursuit of peace. Power is the biggest life mission for almost everyone. In such situation, conflicts are usual. But they should not be dealt with the same usual manner. Some unusual tricks and strategies can be employed to handle conflict. Cooperation or cooperative efforts can help handle conflict. Conflict takes place where there is a matter of ego, temper or disagreements. Such problems need intellectual involvements. Some internal dialogue may help understand the real form and reason for the conflict. Such analytical exercises can make drastic changes in the places, relations and matters where conflict exists.

Complaining Vs Complimenting

It has been seen that some employees have habits of complaining. Their complains range from the government sector to the street shop counters. Such people have the habit of highlighting the flaws and ignoring strengths. Such people complain for the thorns in a rose bush and forget the fragrant and vibrant flower of rose that blossoms ignoring the thorns around. A complaining person is generally ignorant about positive aspects that are associated with the subject of complaint. We have heard a proverb, "No one is perfect". It also means "everyone is imperfect in one or the other manner". The negative aspects of complaining nature can harm the relations. Contrary to complaining, complimenting can create wonders. To compliment a colleague on his achievement is to notice his/her positive side. Such gestures create a spiral of positive energy around both, the giver and the receiver and eventually this positive energy surround the office.

Separating Vs Mobilising

A corporate house is an amalgamation of a heterogeneous group of employees who have different aims, different strategies and techniques to achieve those aims, also different temperaments and different managerial skills. The irony is that heterogeneous group works together, under the same roof and same rules and regulations. However, their priorities, preferences and prejudices create some dividing lines that further takes the form of favouritism and groupism. Such groupings are unhealthy for the growth of the employees as well as the organisations. Any such divides should not be promoted and the leaders as well as the employees should put in required efforts to transform the separating environment into the mobilising one. Collective efforts create scope for intellectual exchange, mutual benefit and a modest environment that becomes instrumental in the growth of the employee as well as the organisation.

Having stated these ten negative and positive aspects of Office Politics, it is imperative to state that to be positive is not to be meek and subdued. To obey the seniors is not to compromise with the self-respect. Politeness does not teach timidity and voicelessness. Smart and skilful dedication helps an employee to create an image of repute. One needs to be honest to the work and the workplace. An humble employee should keep a check lest the humbleness is not becoming the subject of humiliation. Self-centeredness and self-effacement; both should be avoided. The key take away here is to inculcate a "balanced nature". This reminds the advice of Father Polonius to Son Laertes in Shakespearean tragedy *Hamlet*.

Give thy thoughts no tongue,
Nor any unproportioned thought his act.

Be thou familiar, but by no means vulgar.

Those friends thou hast, and their adoption tried,
Grapple them to thy soul with hoops of steel;
But do not dull thy palm with entertainment
Of each new-hatch'd, unfledged comrade. Beware
Of entrance to a quarrel, but being in,
Bear't that the opposed may beware of thee.
Give every man thy ear, but few thy voice;
Take each man's censure, but reserve thy judgment.
Costly thy habit as thy purse can buy,
But not express'd in fancy; rich, not gaudy;
For the apparel oft proclaims the man,
And they in France of the best rank and station
Are of a most select and generous chief in that.
Neither a borrower nor a lender be;
For loan oft loses both itself and friend,
And borrowing dulls the edge of husbandry.
This above all: to thine ownself be true,
And it must follow, as the night the day,
Thou canst not then be false to any man.

Polonius' advise should be taken by all who are aspiring and ambitious to earn good name in the professional world. If one is true to his/her self, there would neither be any chance of being disrespectful towards others nor making any compromise with self respect.

Recognize the Workplace Personalities Beyond Biodata:

In the previous section we have studied how positive energy can defeat office politics and make the office culture more amiable and encouraging to work and grow. In addition, for an aspiring employee it is equally important to recognise the workplace personalities. This knowledge about the colleague is beyond his/her biodata. It is more about the basic nature that is crucial in affecting the work ambience either positively or negatively. Let us study ten major personalities who are often seen in organisations and who actively influence the work culture.

Office Personalities

1. Goal-Oriented
2. Encouraging
3. Sensitive
4. Opportunist
5. Patronising
6. Non-technical
7. Gossip-lover
8. Bullying
9. Fake
10. Trend setter

Goal Oriented – The Natural Purifier

A goal oriented employee is a complete package of almost all the positive characteristics that an organisation needs. Goal orientation teaches excellent planning, decision making, time management and analytical abilities. With these qualities, the employee can never be distracted, unproductive or mundane. Such personalities keep on achieving the milestones on the path of their career. They don't teach or preach anything by words. Their involvement in their work and engagement in progressive activities is so powerful that no distracting energies can affect them. Their analytical abilities and logical reasoning help them think critically and work diligently. With these potential aptitude, such personalities make the maximum use of the available resources. Goal oriented personalities are the assets to the organisation. The reason behind it is that such personalities are always optimistic and so develop the skills to transfer every despairing matter into an opportunity to learn a new skillset and to achieve a new milestone. They smartly differentiate between criticism and concerns. They set the bar of success so high that others would surely feel encouraged to work hard to set their goals. It would not be wrong to say that they are the natural purifiers who inevitably remove every kind of extra burden and botheration. It is in profit to a junior employee to work under the able guidance of such goal oriented personalities. This type of personalities teach their juniors/interns at direct and indirect levels. Directly they teach how to carry out the responsibilities and indirectly they teach how to prioritise the work and how to value time, finance and energy.

Encouraging – The Natural Filters

Encouragement boosts one's morale and confidence to work hard. Those who encourage others, speak through their experiences. They hone up others' skills to be more inclusive in the work culture. They have passed through many ups and downs in their work lives, so have learnt the lesson of success through many trials and errors. The encouraging people share their experience unrestrictedly so that others can overcome the self effacing feelings and be more contributive with optimistic mindset. Sometimes, these people are misunderstood as sympathy gainers whereas they are actually empathetic towards others. To instil courage into others one needs to be more courageous. The encouraging people are kind at heart. Their visionary abilities make them almost like a coach on a ground who pushes the players to perform to take up the challenges and carve out the path to success. In so doing, the encouraging people actually force others to discover their dormant and hidden potential. Their authenticity over their guidance helps others to magnify their talent and pursue their dreams. The encouraging people are honest to their emotions. They are blunt in both criticism and appreciation. Its not possible to manipulate their truthfulness and so their presence, in a way, controls the possibility of discrimination or appeasement. Their positivity affects many in an organisation. Such people are assets to the organisation. They are the natural filters who drain the negative emotions and establish a positive ambience of morality and ethics.

Sensitive – The Unique

To be sensitive is a virtue. It speaks for the pure heart and mind. But a workplace demands practicality, practical approach towards the office matters. Sensitive people are unknowingly exclusive. Their presence demands attention. They have a unique art to seek attention. They are true to their emotions, they are uncut diamonds and so they need to be handled with care. Most of the time, the sensitive people are off track, they think from heart. Mind games are not their forte. Yet, they are not less in any level of contribution. Their intelligence or work efficiency is not to be underestimated. They are hardworking, punctual and law abiding. They are polite and honest and want others to be the same. Thus, they treat all with special care and expect the same from others. Their heart is full of love and compassion and so they don't appreciate if others are practical or calculative. It will not shock us to note that a small lie becomes a matter of deceit to them. They are respectful in the organisation but they are vulnerable to any emotional damage. These people are on a higher level of spiritualism. They carry a good amount of spiritual knowledge and so they relate more with the spiritual and not with the mechanical art of living. Thus, sensitive people, despite their virtues and abilities, lack professionalism and so generally they are left out in the mainstream activities of the organisation.

Opportunist – A Guest Entry

The opportunists are smart, clever and self-centred, in a way they are selectively alert. The opportunists appear only when they find their profit. Greed and selfishness are the driving forces to the opportunists. They are smart to take advantage of others' hard work. If they take a lead role in some joint project, they are inactive almost till the moment of the final presentation. They would call a meeting, take the progress report from others, make presentations and would incur praise as well as incentive from the boss. They believe in making guest entries and thus stealing attention and praise from the boss. They are wrong not in professional matters but in their personal-ethical manners. Opportunism does not affect the growth of the organisation but it surely affects the personal terms and the work ambience. Such people keep others negatively engaged. Others would put in extra efforts to hide personal or official matters from the opportunists. In a way, opportunists promote smart and swift decision-making abilities of the co-workers. They also challenge the role of a leader or a supervisor who has to be careful about disseminating work and duties, keeping a track of work completion and finally acknowledging the dedication of an employee who is consistently involved in carrying out the work.

Patronising: Difficult Dealers

Patronising people are decent in appearance and so their suggestions, guidance, instructions or advises are accepted without any doubt. However, it is better to check whether they are really caring and concerned or just wish to inflict the power of superiority over others. Patronising people are actually self-surrounded by their seniority status and so they try to keep an upper-hand over the juniors for personal satisfaction. Such people take extra liberty in making belittling comments that morally discourage and instil a kind of inferiority feeling in others. They make it a point to be noticed for their interventions in every matter. Their knowledge sharing and advises can be helpful but their "know-all" attitude completely undermines others' participation. Thus, their intentions are always under question. It becomes difficult to deal with them. The other employees can avoid frequent contact with the patronising people. To avoid any clash or contentions, the employees can manage to control the patronisers by reflecting a composed body language and non-verbal signals of inattentiveness. Such smart tactics can reduce their over intimacy generated out of their superiority feelings. Over and beyond, patronising affects the learning curve of the employees so it is advisable to keep safe distance from them.

Non-Technological – Sweet Liability

We are living in a digitalised world. Technology has swept into our daily lives. The present time of Covid-19 Pandemic has made us more technological and digitalised. From admissions to exams, from shopping to competing, and from advance booking/registering to gifting; by and large all the activities are being done through cashless economy. E-banking/net banking has changed the living standards today. In this situation, it is an unproclaimed mandate to be technically smart to survive in a corporate culture. Nevertheless, there are some who are resistant to adopt the digital mode of transactions and transmissions. They are hesitant to get adapted to this 'new normal'. Such colleagues appear passive and unenergetic in the organisation. They are always looking for the help of others. Their conventional attitude make their services almost redundant. Such colleagues should upgrade themselves digitally. In the present times, technological equipment and methods evolve day in and day night. The services of the non-technical people will go unnoticed and unacknowledged if they do not subscribe to the changing terms and conditions of the corporate life. It will not be wrong to say that the non-technical people turn out to be dependants and so they remain clueless about the basic operating system and always need some help from the technical people.

Gossip-Lover – The Busy Bee

Gossip lovers are the busy bees who labour a lot to collect news and information from every corner of the office and then they distribute according to the situation and matters. It is their natural instinct to roam around all the cabins or cubicles and show interest in almost everything. These people have a habit of digging out all the matters for no reason. Their rolls vary from that of detectives to onlookers to observers to sweeteners and also to spoilers. They are anxious to know everything about their colleagues. To a certain level, they influence others also by their variegated gossip sharing. It is important for others to recognise and discourage them at the very outset. Their friendship may portray others also in the same light. It is very necessary to understand that gossip mongers waste their as well as others' productive time. The irony is that there cannot be any punishment for gossiping. At the most, they become subject to others' disrespect and dislike. It is in extreme cases of registered complains that these people may be reprimanded and/ or also terminated if their gossip is found at the centre of any big clash or conflict.

Bullying-The Rude Ones

To bully someone is to bury his/her self-respect and moral courage. The bullies are rude and harsh towards others. The new entrants focus more on profile making and try to avoid any clash or conflict that can damage their career. The bullies target them for their sadistic pleasures and pressurise them to work for them. Sexual harassment is the most heinous form of bullying. Though most of the organisations have anti-harassment cell that takes care of such sensitive issues, the amount of such cases does not recede. Through news channels or newspapers or even around us we can see the presence of the bullies. With the rise of social media, cyberbullying is also rampant. Such people must be punished with extreme severity. The victim must gather courage to file an official complaint against such people. The organisation head also take the severe action against the bullies. Treating them with any kind of liberal approach would harm the office environment and the brand name too. Every employee, whether new or experienced, they must put their foot down against the bullies. The employees should remove the fear of incurring problems for entering into any kind of confrontation with them. With the weapons of courage and clarity, the monster of bully can be handled.

Fake – The Bluff-Master

Qualities of lying, hiding, deceiving instigating, colliding etc. are generally seen in the fake people. They wear a mask of generosity and supportiveness whereas their main focus remains on damaging others repute, relationship or job profile. The biggest challenge in dealing with such people is that they are not easily identified. Also, they carry out their plans with extra cleverness and planning so it is difficult to identify them. They are inconsistent about their actions, behaviour and words. They win others' trust with their sugar-coated language. It is difficult to separate their words from their intentions. The only way to recognise them is to control them with witty arguments, by counter-questioning and by dragging them in deep conversations and thus force them to give analytical clarifications. In short, by making them uncomfortable with a demand of justification for whatever they say. Plain and simple conversation would promote their fake nature. Their bluff-mastery will not be resisted unless they are put down and caught red-handed. Strategic communication is the only way to trap the fake people in their own verbal tangles of double-faced personality.

Trend Setter: The All-Rounders

Trend setters are the complete packages of almost all the positive aspects of the workplace personalities. They have confidence in themselves. Their approach towards work, co-workers and work culture is decent, impressive and influential. Their diligence and skilfulness is appreciated and also followed by the co-workers. They are always well-dressed, well-mannered and well-focused. Their decency may be original or it may be adopted as a strategy to work without any conflict or controversy. Trend setters can be seen at any level, they can be juniors, seniors, managers or Chief Executive Officers or Managing Directors. Mostly, trend setters top the priority list of any organisations as they have engaging as well as appealing set of 3Ps – potential, performance and personality. They are highly spirited and self-driven. Such qualities positively affect the co-workers from millennials to Generations X and Y. The 3Ps of the trend setters can also be used during any workplace conflict or crisis. These unique qualities promote the trendsetters to higher positions. Trend setters think out of the box. The head of the organisation must recognise their innovative approaches at the earliest and accordingly encourage and facilitate them. Their energy, enthusiasm, work effectively and affirmative behaviour is in the profit of the organisation. It is the responsibility of the organisation management to recognise the worth of such workers and invest in them for more future profit.

Corporate House: A Mosaic

As discussed, office politics is the most deliberate topic to talk about. It is unavoidable as well as un-ignorable. It exists in its most sophisticated form. It is intangible and so it makes the situation more vulnerable. Office politics takes place when the employees on the horizontal line face some differences or discriminations and try to approach the seniors in the vertical line. There are umpteen numbers of reasons when the employees feel that they are neglected. These reasons maybe genuine or may be fabricated. Some of them are:

1. Salary Differences
2. Appraisal Delay
3. Lack of Verbal Encouragement
4. Deliberate Avoidance
5. Preference to Others
6. No Grievance Redressal Cell
7. No Promotional Ranking
8. Gossip
9. Lack of Transparency
10. No Moral Boosting

These are just a few to count. We know that every mind is a world and every world is unique. There are some who work hard and some who hardly work. Every corporate house faces this mosaic tile that is so variegated and yet a unit whole. Some employees are jealous, some are short tempered and some believe in appeasement and some are relatives/friends of the Boss so they get maximum chances to escalate the ladder of success. All these characteristic features and their consequences are called, in corporate language as, office politics. Office politics is visible yet not curable, removable and replaceable. Nevertheless, one should not forget that Office Politics is controllable, manageable and thus also tameable.

With a view to control Office Politics, one needs to find out the office personalities. Majorly there are two types of basic personality traits that can be seen around us. They are positive and negative. These are the personalities that are naturally engaged in creating or destroying the image of the office, respectively.

Positive Personalities:

1. Motivators
2. Helpers
3. Supporters
4. Advisors
5. Responsive
6. Sharing
7. Agreeable
8. Approachable
9. Sociable
10. Kind

Negative Personalities:

1. De-motivators
2. Toxic
3. Attention Seekers
4. Short tempered
5. Arrogant
6. Spoilers
7. Unapproachable
8. Adamant
9. Self-centred
10. Jealous

The positive personalities are assets to the workplace and the negatives are the parasites.

One works as engine and the other as boggy.

The first is asset and the latter is liability.

One takes care of the brand image and the other fails to pay due respect to the company's brand.

One thinks about mutual benefit, the other is self-centric.

One is approachable, the other is restrictive.

One gives solutions, the other creates problems.

Thus, the list can go on and on. But professionalism is more about taking care of the mind over heart. One who controls the level of anxiety, irritation, frustration, aggression and chooses peace over turbulence; becomes a model performer for others. Almost everyone knows that negative spiral mars the inner being and also the outer world. Negative people, though unaware of their mental state, also sometimes wish to kick the bucket of negativity but their natural instinct creates hindrance. Such people, when they get a touch of positivity from their colleagues, their job performance is noticeably changing into a bright side. Positivity is effective as well as affective.

It is generally believed that over sensitive people are not professional. However, those who are self-centred, bitter and sadist are more unprofessional. If inadequacy is not professionalism, so is malicious smartness. It is the leader who establishes transparency and promotes professionalism at workplace. There is big 'no' for favouritism and groupism, if one wants to establish a professional ambience.

We all want to live a meaningful life. A life that is devoid of conflict, clashes, contradictions, and also competitions. We all dream for a peaceful life, at social as well as professional level. We all are a pack of limitations and strength, goodness and flaws, abilities and inabilities, aspirations, desires, dreams and agility to accomplish them. Some of us get the expected results, others continue their journey. But in so doing, we forget to monitor ourselves lest we do not compromise with our value ethics. Here comes the role of **Workplace Ethics** – a concept and a practical tool to detox all the impurities hiding under the personal, psychological, social and professional self. According to Abraham Maslow's hierarchy of needs model, as given here, physiological need is at the base and self-actualisation is at the top of the model.

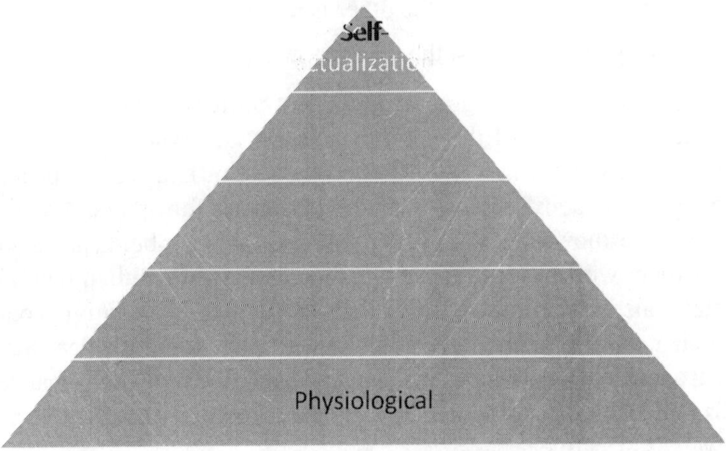

Figure 7: Abraham Maslow's Hierarchy of Needs.

According to the model, self-actualisation is the ultimate need for any human being. It means, every human being is incomplete if the ultimate stage of need is not attained. With the help of Maslow's model, the employees and employers, both should respect each other's structure of need. And under the practice of downward communication, an employer should acquaint the employees with the hierarchical structure of need and should also protect the horizontal and vertical line of the employees.

Multi-Dimensional Workplace Environment

Gone are the days to argue or debate over the living style that is fast and furious. We are a way away from the most loved slow motion of the ethnic life that we could manage to keep alive, roughly, upto the middle of the nineteenth century. The ethnic flavour and fervour is still not completely lost but it would not be wrong to say that its sparse presence is felt either in memories or in museums. Today, the world works around the clock and aptly understands the general wisdom of the adage, "time and tide waits for none".

The over absorbing rapidity of life is reluctant to give any break. Time and again we excuse ourselves from duties and responsibilities by using the all-pertinent common dictum, "I don't have time". Somewhere in our minds, we mistake this excuse for panacea. We forget about the concept of time-management; things get accumulated and we fail to complete the daily circle of duty and responsibility. Nevertheless, it is surprising to notice that even in the recurrent hullabaloo of the heavily loaded life, the reverence for prayer is unconditionally unaffected. Yes, of course, the modes of prayer offering and recitation are somewhat changed. One recites prayers while taking bath, getting ready for office, driving or riding car or two-wheeler; or while cooking, dusting, cleaning or travelling. The focal point here is to see how a regular order of prayer recitation can help create a warm and decent work culture. Unfortunately, such recitation is, sometimes a habitual affair or an unconscious and duty-bound chanting. What one needs is to understand the words of the prayers and see whether the meaning of the prayer is protected by the behaviour. The vedic *sutras* – aphorisms from Vedas like *Satyam vad, Dharmam char, swadhyayan ma pramaditavyam* translated respectively as speak truth, be dutiful, do not be lethargic in observing your regular learning-lessons – should be used as touchstones to check the vulnerability of an individual and collective behaviour. The understanding of such sutras creates positivity in the ambiance.

Social conduct is more about the behaviour expected by the society than by an individual. Let us put these two into a tabular form and see where is a scope to fill in the gap, if there is any.

A Behaviour Expected on Workplace	B Personal -Choice Based Behaviour
Vocality	Silent
Society centric	Self centric
Collective concern	Individual concern
Sharing	Hiding
Team work	Working as individual
Open ended behaviour	Close ended behaviour
Inclusivity	Exclusivity

Behaviour is the result of the nature of a person. Some prefer to work from silos, with their self-designed work ambiance and team. But it is quite opposite to the workplace expectation where being collective and inclusive is the central force. When personal behaviour goes against the expected behaviour, the positive energy goes missing.

The gap between real and expected behaviour can be filled in by proper understanding followed by active implementation of prayers in our day to day life. For most of the service class workers, a day is broadly divided into two halves: 9:00 A.M. to 6:00 P.M. and 6:00 P.M.to 9:00 A.M.: the first time-unit is completely dedicated to the workplace whereas the second is for family, friends and extended relations. Furthermore this time unit has a non-active zone of 6 to 8 hours sleep. This time division shows that our longer period of active engagement is with the workplace where productive consistency results into growth of the individual and also the company/organisation that one is associated with.

As workplace takes the major part of our concentration, time and contribution; a small psychological disturbance may affect one's productive performance. The workplace culture and structure need friendliness horizontally (among employees) and vertically (hierarchically). In short, a faithful, reliable, considerate ambience would raise the productivity graph of an individual's career as well as the company's overall growth and repute.

The only remedy to fend off any stress and create a positive spiral around is to routinely recite prayers and understand the associated meaning. The Vedic prayer selected here is familiar to us since the pre-primary school days. The prayer words are: *Om sahna vavatu* (together we two may move). The cluster of two may comprise of the other and the self. In the organisational culture it can be an employee and an employer. The prayer teaches us to perform and prosper together. Our studies lead us to respect each other that further may lead to the spiritual knowledge and finally sets us free from all kinds of hostilities. What we need and should pray for is **PEACE**, within and without. The central idea of this prayer is togetherness. It reminds the proverb, "together we stand divided we fall". Good relations at workplace make work more enjoyable that can provide sufficient scope for accommodating innovative ideas as well as creative zeal. Faith in the individual talent, respect for the other's potential, mindful behaviour, readiness for change, open ended communication and smooth interactions help build good relations at workplaces.

The present time workplace environment comprises of four major components:

1. Multicultural
2. Competitive
3. Hierarchical, and
4. Unpredictable.

Multicultural

It is an accepted truth that the world is a global village. The credit for the same goes to the incessant flow of migration, across the national and international borders. The ongoing process of migration has made the world culturally, religiously and linguistically inclusive and also absorbing. The present time corporate world is highly multicultural and thus creates a space for mutual relations among the employees. This provides a pretty good space to exchange the interpersonal skills to communicate, socialise, connect and co-operate. With the help of these acquired skills, the employees can develop good rapport among each other which is eventually beneficial to the growth of the company.

Competitive

The corporate world today is competitive where every employee aims higher for a brighter prospect. The term 'competition' needs a sincere attention as it may result into either creative or destructive situation. If competition is interpreted with a touch of honesty and dignity for work, the progress of a colleague becomes the matter of inspiration and not of jealousy. One has to keep a check on his/her ability and dedication to the work assigned. Competitiveness actually instils the passion to grow and rise at workplaces. Competitive people are aware of their strength and weakness and so employ themselves accordingly. Nevertheless, stress is a sure gift of competitiveness that may hamper an individual's spiritual progress. Stress from competitiveness can be managed provided the competitor takes judicious and not impulsive decisions.

Hierarchical

The work structure of every corporate house is hierarchical. Simply put, it is a game of giving and taking orders. Here, Freudian idea of tripartite triggers of personality as reflected through Id, Ego and Superego has all the possible chances to pop up and affect/damage the work as well as the relations. These three components of personality carry a relative impression to the work, worker and the workplace. The top-down hierarchy should be avoided as the distinct hierarchical structure affects the positive flow of energy and thoughts. At some organisations, the boss feels free to prepare an afternoon green tea or espresso coffee for the colleagues; though it may not be always. A down to earth behaviour of a boss and the obedient colleagues on horizontal line is more productive than the old school hierarchical mentality.

Unpredictable

One needs to prepare for an abrupt change in the workplace environment, though it happens rarely. There are possibilities for the unpronounced changes and shifts in the functional pattern of a workplace. We know that every new regime brings in new changes that demand new skill sets and strategies to overcome any shock. In such situation, when the changes are drastic and affect every employees, one must not take it personally. The only key to handle this unpredictable change is to stay updated with the latest knowledge and remain tied to value system. If one is ethical, duty-bound and committed to the responsibilities; there will be less chances to get affected with any change or shift at the workplace. A balanced mind works with consistent positivity even in an adverse situation.

Workplace Spirituality

Workplace Spirituality is nothing but understanding the core value of the adage "work is worship". A German proverb speaks, "A clean conscience is the best pillow". Workplace life would be more zealous, productive and inspiring if spirituality is expressed through our work behaviour and maintained in the work culture.

One axiom we need to accept that the society that we live in is made up by us. The society's beliefs, justice, evils, ill practices etc., are the byproducts of our own mismanagement and misconduct with the divine order. Finn Collin says,

> The notion of *homo faber,* man the toolmaker, has iconic significance in our culture: human beings devise tools and, in using them to create and transform their environment, they make of the natural realm in which they evolved as a species a new order, one brought into being and sustained by themselves.[1]

The rudimentary tools that we made to protect us or the machines that we invented to facilitate us have taken away many inherent skills and crafts from us. The human proximity and warmth is also shrinking and receding. But this is the beauty of modern world. We cannot survive without the facilities around us. The only need is to understand the knowledge of the self that respects the other human being with zeal and positivity that can be attained through Five Cs.

Clarity,

Cooperation,

Compassion,

Coherence and

Cordiality.

These quality assets would build a harmonious work culture. If the root of a workplace culture is nourished with these five Cs, the workers would be successful and progressive.

In an opening verse of the *Astavakra Samhita*, the sage Astavakra sums up all the prerequisites to spiritual liberation as follows: If you aspire after liberation, shun the objects of the senses as poison and seek forbearance, sincerity, kindness, contentment, and truthfulness as nectar. Like all proper systems of self-inquiry, Advaita Vedanta lays down four prerequisites or qualities for a seeker after Self-knowledge, as follows:

1. Discrimination—*viveka*—between the real and the unreal
2. Renunciation—*vairagya*—of the unreal
3. Six Virtues/Treasures—*shatsampatti*—of self-control
4. Longing for liberation—*mumukshuta*

Though these are the prerequisite qualities of a seeker, they would surely help constructing a convivial office ambience if developed as a form of workplace culture. Life at workplace is mostly spent under a threat, threat to employee's competency, efficiency, longevity and remittance. The dynamic work life needs integration of the individual's ambitions, aspirations, the driving force and the availability of the resources and the surroundings. It is not about compromising with the situation or signing a low profit deal but it is about thoroughly examining the facilitator points and determining points. Workplace career is by and large a sum total of innumerable examinations like this. In this game of "wish to win", the result is unpredictable. An employee is thus advised to draw a line of distinction between private-life and public-life to strike a balance between home and office and thus to create a peaceful personality that can self-evaluate the performance without any preference or prejudice. Such personality can clearly identify the right path to follow. One needs to be free of the acronym FEAR that stands for Fight, Ego, Anxiety and Retain and one needs to develop the same acronym for Forgive, Embrace, Agility and Relieve.

- Fight or Forgive
- Ego or Embrace
- Anxiety or Agility
- Retain or Relieve

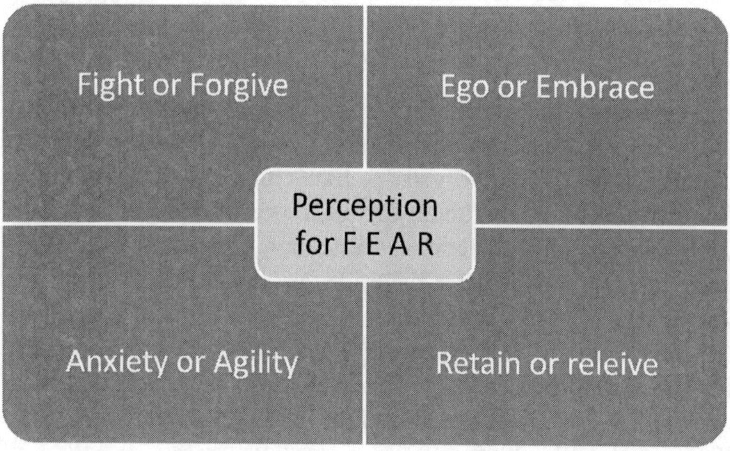

Source: Author's Presentation.

Figure 8: Perception for F E A R.

The word 'FEAR' speaks for our nervous system. FEAR can be handled by changing our perception for it. Here is an attempt made to understand the acronym F E A R with a new, fresh and positive perspective. If we have fear of fight, ego, anxiety or of retaining negative feelings; we should make efforts to replace these negative feelings with the positive feelings like forgiving, embracing, being agile for change and feeling relieved of mental burden. We can clearly distinguish the gravity of the first from the other. Forgiving a friend, embracing his follies or weakness, being agile towards commitments and relieving the unnecessarily incurred stress would be far better and profitable than fighting over a petty issue. Being egoist and creating a glass ceiling around or being anxious and retaining the burden over the mind and heart would make the work life more stressful.

Adi Guru Shankaracharyaji writes in *Vivekchudamani,*

Ahmkarhs vigneyh karta bhoktabhimanyayam

Satvadigunyogen chavasthatray mashnute,

Know that it is the ego which, identifying with the body, becomes the doer or the experience and in conjuction with the Gunas such as Sattava etc., this ego assumes the three different states (of waking, dreaming and deep sleep). Vivekchudamani 104

Ego affects three stages of our life; waking, dreaming and deep sleep. It possesses us in the web of self-surroundedness. This web blindfolds us from the virtues like empathy and sympathy. Sunirmalananda writes about six virtues/treasures of self-control. These virtues form the ethical foundation of spiritual life. Their practice prepares the inner faculties for the cultivation of higher knowledge. These virtues are: (a) *Sama*: control of the mind; (b) *Dama*: control of the senses; (c) *Uparati*: equanimity of mind; (d) *Titiksha*: forbearance; (e) *Samadhana*, concentrating the mind on Truth; and (f) *Sraddha*: active faith in the teacher and scriptures (Sunirmalananda, 2005).

With these virtues, one can detach the self from all the futile engagements; one can develop the highest code of conduct. Such a person is loyal, kind and calm. These virtues work as the guiding force that establishes serenity around him/her. For such an enlightened person, decision taking ability, core competency and also courageous aptitude is *sahaj,* natural. Such a person has the *abhamandal* aura around him/her that results into the source of inspiration to others. Such an individual maintains standards which provide guidance and courage to understand and respect the subtle connections of the world in relation to his or her life. An honest person appreciates the interconnectedness of the natural world and does not misuse, abuse, or waste the wealth of resources provided for the well-being of humanity. An honest person does not take for granted his or her own resources such as mind, body, wealth, time, talents, or knowledge. Honesty means never to misuse that which is given in trust. Imagine a workplace where virtues like honesty, sincerity, respect, faith and generosity are powerfully established and a positive spiral is created that evades every kind of negative energy.

Dr. Radhakrishnan has said, if we exclude spiritual training from our institution we would be untrue to our whole civilisation. Indian civilisation has always advocated work ethics. We have ethical scriptures like Chanakya Neeti, Vidur Neeti and also Shukra Neeti. Our Vedas, Smritis, Samhitas, Upanishads, Aranyakas, Purans and the Epics have always taught the lawful *–neetiyukt* behaviour at every stage of our life. The ancient Indian literature of wisdom has framed a rule book for kings, ministers, advisors, pundits and also the workers. Ancient wisdom literature gives many examples that work as touchstones to the present day work culture.

The twenty first shloka of Chapter 16th from Bhagvad Geeta reads:

TrividhamNarkasyedamdwaramnaashanmaatmanah
Kamahkrodhasthathalobhastasmaadetattrayam tyajet.

(Lust, anger and greed are the three doors of Hell. So, shun them for your spiritual growth).

This shloka bears testimony to the general wisdom for righteous behaviour. Lord Krishna, the charioteer of Arjuna from the Epic-song of Bhagvad Geeta, is the lawful political advisor who lists out how humans can learn the eternal law of righteousness and how they can live a peaceful and fruitful life by being honest in their lives. The same advice is applicable for a better, higher and satisfying work-life.

The relationship between an employer and an employee is based on loyalty, trust, faith and mutual respect. Spirituality at workplace is nothing but the respect that both can nurture for each other. No work-life is devoid of challenges. But one sure-fire thing that the both need to understand is that the *problem* is the challenge and not the *person*. Once this fundamental understanding of the spiritual aspect of the workplace is developed, the human energy would focus more on the problem/crisis/conflict and would make all the conscious efforts to fight them out and establish a peaceful ambience at workplace.

According to the Sustainable Development Goal No. 8 "Decent Work and Economic Growth", any organisation should mainly focus at promoting unrelenting, inclusive and sustainable economic growth by providing full and productive employment and decent work and work culture to all. Spiritual awareness that covers mental as well being and good health can play prime role in transforming a stressed work life into a decent. The following prayers teach to establish harmony in the human society.

ॐ सहनाववतु
सहनौभुनक्तु
सहविरयैकरवावहै
तेजस्विनावधीतमस्तु
माविदविषावहै
ॐ शांतिशांतिशांति।[1]

Together may we two move,
Together may we two relish,
Together may we two perform,
May what has been studied by us be (filled with the) brilliance (of understanding) leading to knowledge, (and)
May it not give rise to hostility (due to lack of understanding)
Om! Peace! Peace! Peace!

Recitation of such prayers help reduce the levels of inequality and any emotional insecurity and establish harmony among the colleagues. Alongwith prayers and all the spiritual sensibilities related to the knowledge over life purpose and active community engagements, effective communication skills also play a vital role in making the workplace landscape harmonious, productive, decent and sustainable.

Barriers Effective Communication Skills

Communication is a two way process that involves a speaker and a listener who share their ideas. This sharing is considered complete when the idea of a speaker is conveyed to the listener so very effectively that the latter either accepts, rejects, counters or shows doubt regarding the same. In short, the listener's response gives a final touch to the communication. This *final touch* is known as feedback in the process of communication. We can also say that the speaker encodes a meaning in a word/sentence, the listener decodes the same meaning and responds to the decoded meaning. This response is called as feedback of the process of communication.

The expected feedback may not be received if there is noticed any discrepancy in either encoding or decoding the message. This discrepancies are known in the corporate world as **Barriers to Effective Communication**. These barriers are:

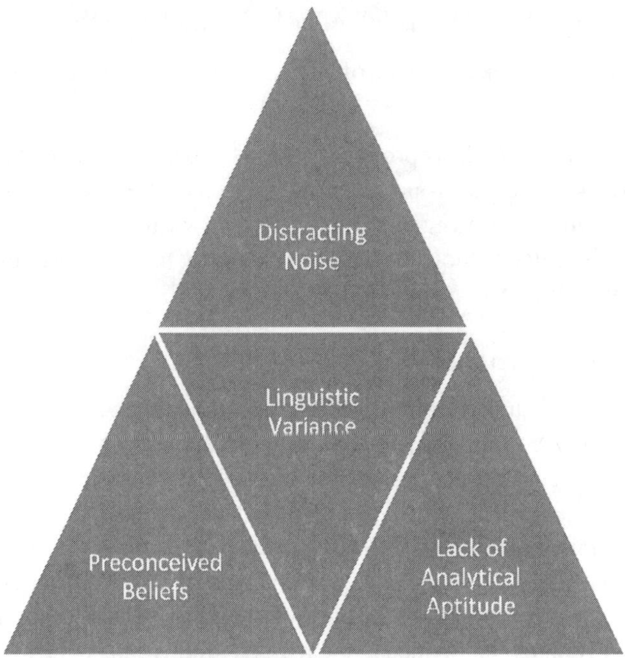

Source: Authors' representation.

Figure 9: Linguistic Variance.

Distracting Noise

This takes place when it is a matter of oral communication. A speaker and a listener both are comfortable to speak and hear respectively at a moderate pitch. If a speaker speaks louder than the natural pitch of sound, there are chances of getting diverted, drained and disordered while encoding and decoding the message. Some unnecessary noise during the process of communication also works as barrier to effective communication. Such noises are, barking of dogs, honking of vehicles, hooting and shouting of children, processions with loud music, machine drilling or any sudden interfering explosion etc. Such noise are capable enough to upset the communication process. Sometimes, lack of pronunciation clarity can also mar the chain of communication. For example:

If a person pronounces lake as lack and says,

Thoreau's Walden is full of lacks (instead of lakes). Or

Due to the lake (in stead of lack) of water, life in village became difficult.

The word 'lack' is pronounce with the broad sound of 'a' and the word 'lake' is pronounced with the narrowed sound of 'a'. While mispronouncing one with the other, the meaning gets disrupted. Such disruptions badly affect the process of communication.

Linguistic Variance

For a smooth and meaningful communication, the code of language needs to be one and the same between the speaker and the listener. Effective communication is not possible if the speaker speaks in a language that the listener is not aware of. For effective communication both need to be on same page as far as the language is concerned. This can be seen in the role of idioms in language. Idioms are rooted in the culture of the land. And so they have cultural context embedded in them. Such idioms can not be directly translated into any other language. For example,

Do not put all eggs in one basket. This American idiom carries an advice to safely invest money at more than one places so that if one place of investment turns out to be unsafe, the remaining amount is not affected. This idiom shares a piece of wisdom as far as investment is concerned. But in a vegetarian region, or rather a region when eating egg is almost a sacrilege, the use of the same idiom will surely remain misinterpreted. Effective communication is not possible with the same linguistic code between the speaker and the listener.

Preconceived Beliefs

It is more than necessary to keep the mind open for suggestions, advices, guidance or any intellectual proposal for personal as well as organisational growth. Preconceived beliefs may block the chance to the same. Any judgemental decision can surely affect the effectiveness of the communication. If a speaker is hypercritical or over impressed about the listener, he may end up encoding/decoding the message and thus the effective communication is disrupted.

Lack of Analytical Aptitude

This can be considered as the extension of the preconceived beliefs. Whether a person is hypercritical or over-impressed by the other, there is high possibility that he/she reads the messages with tilted glasses. It is an undocumented psychological truth that "love is blind", so is hatred. So blinded by love or hate, jealousy or concern, the analytical aptitude of a person gets affected. Analysis is the backbone of any significant communication. A word and meaning are strongly associated. And for effective communication, one has to take into consideration all the connotative as well as denotative meanings. This is the analytical part to decipher the real meaning embedded in the speeches. Lack of the same may lead to interruption in decoding the meaning from the codes. Unless a detailed examination of the message conveyed or the elements of the structure of the linguistic variety is properly studied one must not jump the gun and reach the conclusion. Such decoding is the result of ignorance and insincerity.

Sometimes self-image or self-concept, whether overrated or underrated, also create hindrance in effective communication. People who are reactive, impatient, poor listeners, short tempered or arrogant would mostly misjudge the situation/person and take a mis-fitting decision.

Incomprehensive Reading

Francis Bacon, the 16th century English essayist says,

> "Reading maketh a full man; conference a ready man; and writing an exact man; and, therefore, if a man write little, he had need have a great memory; if he confer little, he had need have a present wit; and if he read little, he had need have much cunning, to seem to know that he doth not".

According to this quote, Reading is the foundation of the rounded personality. Reading should be done comprehensively and continuously. A well-read person can be easily distinguished as a knowledgeable person. Comprehensive reading is based on Linguistic clarity and Referential Understanding. Absence of these two essential characteristics leads towards miscomprehension of reading.

Communication is the most vital, complex and dynamic process. Every piece of communication carries its uniqueness, specificity and creativity that gets conveyed through the presentability. Communication is in a way an art, some are inherently artistic whereas some need to acquire it. Great speakers like Swami Vivekanand, Abraham Lincoln, Atal Bihari Vajpeyee and also the current Prime Minister of India Shri Narendra Modi are born with great oratory skills. Others may need to learn the skill of communication. These learners may use some Strategic Communication Skills to communicate meaningfully. Let us now study the Strategic Communication Skills.

Notes

1. Collin, F. Social Reality, ebook, https://www.routledge.com/Social-Reality/Collin/p/book/9780415147972 p. 54.

Chapter - 3

Strategic Communication

A strategy is a predesigned, formulated action-plan that is prepared to reach the expected conclusion. It can be an individual or a collective intellectual brainstorming that helps the person to

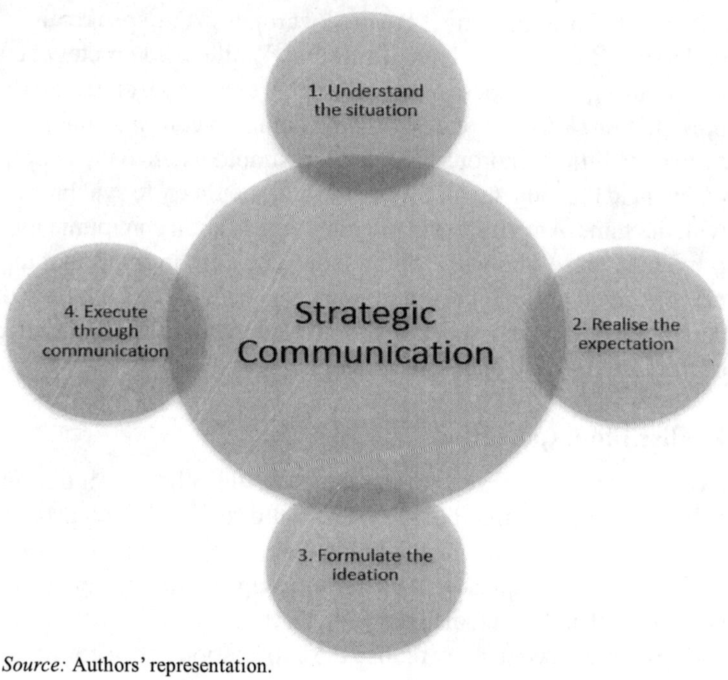

Source: Authors' representation.

Figure 10: Strategic Communication Model.

execute the action systematically and flawlessly. For a noticeable rise in the present time corporate world, a wide ranging exchange of ideas, thoughts, opinions and suggestions should be called for. Strategy is much more than a wish-list. Strategy is equally about the art of excluding the unessential matters that may take away our energy and also efforts. A strategy demands patience, sharpness and right direction. Simply put, strategy is a thoughtful, unbiased and result oriented approach that leads an individual or a team towards the desired success.

Understanding the Situation

This is a primary stage of strategic communication. It is like reading the situation with all awareness and alertness. It is more about the observatory skills. In the professional world, we all are expected to present ourselves with ready wittiness. A slip in reading the situation may prompt the speaker to communicate a misfitting statement. To avoid any such awkwardness, the speaker must understand the place and people around. While in completely new surroundings, the speaker needs to be extra conscious of the presentation skills whereas with some familiar yet formal ambience he may be little humorous. The speaker should listen to the people, understand the topic under discussion and should try to synchronize with the same. Any irrelevant pitching-in may spoil communication flow. One more important point should be kept in mind that any preconceived notion or prejudice can also badly affect the flow of communication. The speaker should understand the importance of the situation and speak accordingly.

Realise the Expectation

Every corporate person holds some or the other designation. While communicating, the speaker should realise the importance of the designation that he/she holds. The sentences should match the stature of the speaker. At a certain stage, every sentence is a commitment and a mutual agreement. During any meeting or formal discussion, everyone must realise the expectation and accordingly speak.

Formulate the Ideation

Communication is a cycle of 3Cs (as discussed earlier) – convey – comprehend – convey. To convey the idea for easy comprehension, the speaker needs to understand how to formulate the flow of communication. When a Director General of any organisation holds the annual meeting, he follows a certain flow of communication. First the DG would

1. Greet the meeting hall/assembly
2. Appreciate the work accomplished
3. May announce some awards
4. Takes suggestions
5. Shares the road-plan for future
6. Shares the expectations from the employees
7. Sets target
8. Thanks and leaves

This flow cannot be maintained if proper ideation is not formulated. Idea is something that connect the past, present and future in one thread of communication. A proper formulation of idea is a key to the successful strategic communication.

Execute with Aplomb

Execution is the last stage of communication that takes care of the thoughts, expectations, targets and future prospects. Execution is successful when a speaker is confident, well researched and well informed. Strategic communication is successful if execution is done flawlessly.

Any strategy in any field or situation is carried out to achieve a target. When a strategy is applied to the process of communication, it becomes strategic communication. Communication in a corporate world is always goal oriented. A corporate communication is never purposeless. Today's corporate world is spread on a global spectrum. International marketing is the key to the economic growth of the world. During the present unprecedented time of Covid-19, we have seen that India took a lead in providing Corona Vaccine to more than 135 countries. According to The Guardian, "India has long been known as the pharmacy of the world" (20th October, 2020). Thus, give and take on an international platform is almost a regular affair in the international marketing. In any such give and take affair in the corporate world, strategic communication is a must.

Strategic communication ranges from a mother making her child eat healthy food to a leader convincing a team to work hard, be focused and stay goal oriented. Some factors can be studied in the given chronological order that help prepare a road map for strategic communication skills with specific focus on the **strategic presentation skills.**

Strategic Presentation Skills

Examination of the Case

While developing strategic communication, one needs to examine the case that is to be introduced, rejected, defended or opposed. Understanding the rationale, applying the proper logic, evaluating the environment, and making a diagnostic study of the whole case helps the communicator to make an impressive presentation. We all know the proverbial sentence, "half knowledge is always dangerous, either be ignorant or be excellent". Half or false knowledge can mar the impression of the presenter as well as that of the corporate house that the person belongs to.

Explicit Knowledge

A case will be examined thoroughly only when the source of the subject is studied explicitly. To gain this source of the knowledge, the presenter needs to organise field investigation, in depth interview/s, or data collection either through offline or online mode. Once an adequate amount of case acquaintance is gained, the actual facts and figures are included in the presentation. Such concrete presentations are impressive as well as benefitting to the company.

The presenter needs to develop an integrating approach to reach the final stage of presentation. The presenter must be open to all the opinions related to the case.

Interactive Transparency

It becomes a responsibility of all engaged in the brainstorming activity to keep interactive transparency. In absence of which, there are high chances of loose threads of communication that further leads the communication to inconclusiveness. Interactive Transparency is established where there is no fear, biasedness, differences and discriminations among the team members.

Team Building

Team building is an art that speaks for the discretionary power of the leader. The task force should be prepared taking into consideration the interest area of the people involved. Some juniors may be employed in such tasks as interns. Their involvement would help themselves as well as the organisation grow and advance.

Effective Leadership

It is the leader under whose able guidance an organisation as well as the employees grow. A leader has to have the inclusive approach towards the employees. A leader's decisive power disseminates the task among the employees. A leader's presence of mind, passion and perseverance affects the team members positively. They look upto the leader as a role model. The time spent with the leader gives chance to the team members to closely observe the leadership qualities. A leader is not a ruler, a leader is a guide who responds patiently to the query of the team members. Yet, the leader does not patronise the team members. A leader has excellent negotiation skills and the ability to recognise the strength and weakness of team members.Though the leader is not actively engaged in carrying out the action plan, he/she remains thoroughly involved in all the activities of the organisation. A leader must know that his/her presence itself can work as moral encouragement to the employees. Thus, a leader is one who leads the team members in particular and the society in general.

Power of Persuasion and Anecdotal Evidences

Strategic communication is also about the power of persuasion, it is an artistic science. Science because it is empirical in nature. To persuade people, one must apply the force of intellectual arguments, exact fact and figure, date and time in case of event description or the number of page and line in case of any reference material to be cited. Such concrete way of communication hardly fails. Such concrete way of communication create a darting, piercing impact on the mind of the listener. Not only that, such communications create a magnificient impression of the speakers. The persuasive talent can make the communication memorable and also historic. We all know Swami Vivekananda's speech at Chicago, where he addressed the World Religion Congress uniquely. Instead of using the most popular salutation, "Ladies and Gentlemen", Swamiji said, "Brothers and Sisters of America". It was such an emotional, honest and impactful address, that the sound of applause continued for more than the usual time. Thus, a persuasive communicator needs to start with an influencing and impactful manner. Such a speakers can easily yet forcefully persuade people.

Budget Clarity

This clarity may not be applicable to every strategic communicator. But in case of marketing, economic clarity remains a focal point of discussion. In cases of promoting your sale or placing orders with quotations, budget clarity makes the communication more concrete and complete. While presenting the budget, the speaker must also include the profit and loss affecting the most junior to the most senior employee of the organisation.

Strategy Formulation and Implementation

Once all these features are studied and examined for the formal communication, the speaker or the team may work on prioritising and arranging the points stepwise. In case of Group Presentation, all the presenters must be aware of flow of the communication. If proper strategy is formed, the team members should know how to avoid parallel speeches and overlapping of ideas. Such internal clarity gives a formal touch to the flow of the presentation. Though communication is an art, it is not rhetoric. The corporate communication is more about Empirical approach and less about the ornamental linguistic beauty. A simple but well-arranged presentation is expected over a verbose and complicated one. When a strategic plan for communication is ready, the team may unanimously decide the stepwise flow of the presentation. This homework is compulsory to make the presentation flawless, impressive and benefitting to the organisation.

Expert Presentation

The most important and final step in the strategic communication is to present it with expertise. An expert presenter is one who is clever, well informed of the matter and a good speaker. Such a strategic communicator creates a pool of information then smartly picks up and assembles the information to make a complete argumentative structure. Such structures are to encourage others to share the innovative ideas and not to build up heated arguments and thus to destroy the ability to work together and succeed. It is the communicator's consistent, candid and clairvoyant behaviour that distinguishes his qualities from others and makes him/her the asset of the organization. It is the one who observes the time limit and wins the attention of the listeners with proficiency of language and impressive eloquence. The expert executor takes all the disagreements healthily and responds to them politely. Such an executor promotes novel ideas and makes the presentation interactive, collaborative and thus builds information network.

This set of 10 characteristic features are the most required qualities to communicate strategically. Strategic communication is a technical communication where the communicator knows the listener's expectations. Accordingly, the speaker plans out the strategy of communication. The expert executor needs to be decisive at times. For this, it is necessary that he/she has consulted the leader prior to the final presentation. This is to avoid any clash or conflict in the future. An expert executor may also employ the tactic of humour. This multiplicity of talent fetches glory to the speaker and also to the organisation. The strategic communicators also prepares a team of highly dedicated employers. Group-thinking or brainstorming become the daily activities between the communicator and the team members. This approach helps the communicator to establish a cords of cordiality and morality to climb the ladders of success for the company, the employees and for the self. There should be fun, openness and broad-mindedness at an organisation. The executive speakers are selected by the leader once the speaker qualifies to earn the title. This would surely distinguish him/her from the other but the same must not become the reason for the speaker's arrogance or exclusiveness. Such features can create the discriminatory lines and make the workplace frustrating, less productive and stressed.

In today's unprecedented time of Covid-19, online mode is the only mean and mode of communication. This is the time when the traditional modes are almost redundant. Along with the technical aspects, the strategic communicator equally needs to be well versed with technological aspects. It may be the future reality that the virtual mode almost replaces the face to face mode. An aspiring communicator must keep an eye on all the nuances associated with the technological aspects related to the communication.

A strategic communicator works in parallel at three levels – administrative, executive and futuristic. The more the investment of time, energy and expertise, the more one reaps the chances for growth and benefit at personal as well as organisational level.

Chapter - 4

Advertisement and Communication

Advertisement – an ACER Tree

An Acer tree is a tree or plant that is often grown for its attractive leaves and bright autumn colours. Advertisements are like the Acer tree; Attractive, Captivating, Engaging and Revealing. Basically, advertisement is used for floating an information that has a direct connection to the human life. Advertisement is an essential tool in marketing. We see advertisements for grocery, stationary, fashion accessory, auto-mobiles, medical stores, hospitals, schools, books, bags, pins, doormats and what not. All these advertisements are prepared with a view to impress and attract a bigger mass of people for better sale and fame. There is no profession, business or even charity trusts that work without advertisements. It is through the medium of advertisements, trade and commerce gets promoted nationally and internationally.

Advertisements and Culture

Language is rooted in the culture of the land and so the language of an advertisement is also selected mindfully that it can attract the people of the culture. The cultural ethos are used with a purpose to connect the product to the culture of the land and thus to attract the consumer-mass belonging to a particular culture. The advertisement of "Cadbury Dairy Milk Chocolate" came up with a promotion of the product as "Celebrations". For that the advertisement shows the Rakshabandhan celebration as a gift of a brother to a sister. This was for the first time a chocolate was used in stead of a sweet. The chocolate wrappers, boxes and hampers are made in extremely designer way. The tag line used says, "Kuch Meetha ho jaye" (let us have some sweets) is a strategy to replace chocolates with sweets. In an advertisement for the "Good Night" mosquitoes controlling machine, a younger brother protects his elder sister from Dengue mosquitoes by switching on the same in the morning, saying that Dengue mosquitoes enter house in the morning. When the sister thanks him for being caring, the younger one says, "ye to mera farz tha" (it was my duty). This sentence introduces Indian culture where a brother, irrespective of the age is supposed to protect the sister. Both these advertisements, expand and give voice to the prominent cultural feature that otherwise remains less attended. The creative team of such advertisements selects the language that doubly impresses the consumer; first by the promotion of cultural ethos and second by showing them occupying the central position in the cultural life. Thus, the advertisements, provide information about the product and leave a mark of influence on the consumer's mind. Such advertisements follow cultural meanings and principles to attract the fundamental aspect of the social life – to stay rooted in the culture. When the consumer finds a correlation between the cultural identity and the product, it is obvious to get attracted towards the advertisement and thus to purchase the product. The cultural manifestation presented through advertisements constitute a world of consumers that remains unaffected by any other gratifying advertisement. The creators of such advertisements study the cultural ethos and accordingly prepare their advertisement for the wider reception. Advertising is an effective medium to promote trade and commerce.

Advertisements and Psychology

Advertisements are impactful when they associate the product with the customer's personal choice criteria of colour, taste, size and shape. Customers, sometimes, buy products only on the basis of colour, size and shape of the package. This is seen more in the products of children. The packages of chips are designed with bright and glossy colours to attract the child customer. Some chocolates like "Kinder Joy" come up with a novel idea of two soft and creamy milky and chocolaty substances with a tiny little spoon and an attractive toy in an oval shape case. When a child opens it, he/she finds a real bundle of joy. Advertisements for 'Tea' would show the lush green tea gardens on the package that endorses the organic purity and thus psychologically impresses customer with a promise to cater to their expectations. Gaudy colours and glossy wrappers/ packages create a psychological pull factor to influence consumers.

Sometimes, decorative arrangements also influence the customers psychologically. This can be seen on the fruit and vegetable lorries or trucks. A heap of green spinach is topped with a red carrot and the bright oranges are arranged in a circular form around green pear. Such decorative arrangement itself advertise the product. The customers would prefer to buy from these well-arranged lorries/trucks than the clumsy unattended heap of fruits/ vegetables, lest it be same in quality and price.

An advertisement is prepared after studying the market behaviour of the consumers. The jingles sung in advertisements remain in the minds of consumers and thus make soft influence over market behaviour. We see almost a flood of advertisement for almost everything and in every sector. There are advertisements that spread awareness about government schemes, projects and funds for public facilities and safety. The constant reminder of the tag line "Do gaj ki doori" (distance of two-three feet) during the time of Covid-19 Pandemic does not allow us to ignore how important it is to maintain distance as a measure of safety and precaution. The slogan lines like "Beti Padhao, Beti Bachao" , "Atmnirbhar Bharat", "Swachch Bharat Abhiyan", and "Vocal for Local". Thus, advertisements use the language of the common people and work as information booth as well as a strong influencer.

Advertisements and History

It is amazing to note how the historical journey of the product becomes a medium to proclaim authenticity, consistency and connectivity. The animated butter-girl Amul was introduced in 1966 as the face of the Amul Dairy Products. This animated girl takes part in almost all the leading stories of the country. The product bags would change her expressions and the status line to show her active presence in the world around.

Source: The Economic Times 4 August, 2020)
https://brandequity.economictimes.indiatimes.com

This status line shows the iconic girl's happiness to see how the Indian superstar of the century returned home defeating the deadly virus Corona. We also see her partaking in almost all the national news either with her witty comments or tongue in cheek humour. The history of Amul and its influencer – the most loved iconic and opinionated animated girl – is very interesting. It was in 1964, The National Dairy Development Board NDDB came out with the dairy development programme for India popularly known as White Revolution. It was the farsightedness of the then General Manager of Amul, Mr. Vergese Kurien who was given the responsibility by the then Indian Prime Minister Shri Lal Bahadur Shastri to promote dairy products in India. The Amul girl is the brain-child of the designer and cartoonist Mr. Jayant Rane. The Amul girl's continuous presence on all the Amul Products never allows us to forget the history of her birth during the historic time of India's "White Revolution".

Advertisements and Art and Aesthetics

The country of India is rich with her aesthetic and artistic values. Indians nurture respect for anything that connects their emotions to Indian Aesthetics, may it be classical dance forms, Karnataki and Hindustani Music, or painting. Our regional languages also connect us with our ancient heritage. Some advertisements use these artistic values and make a strong and persuasive appeal. In one of the advertisements for 'Nestle Kitkat' a Bharatnatyam dancer artistically demonstrates how Kitkat has a particular way to remove the wrapper, cut the chocolaty-waffery bar with the help of a thumb, break the bar from the middle and eat and relish. The speciality of this advertisement is that it does not use any verbal communication. The message is conveyed through non-verbal communication. The most famous artistic ad is by Ustad Jakir Husein who plays tabla, drinks tea and in response to the appreciative line "Wah Ustaad" says "Wah Taj Kahiye". The renowned Tabla player Shri Jakir Husein gives credit to the tea brand Taj. Thus, it is through the innovative methods and manners the advertisements make lasting impressions on the minds of the consumers.

Advertisements and Education

Education is delivered in India through government as well as private institutes. Government and Private Institutes publish educational advertisements in the public interest. These advertisements highlight the special features of the services offered along with the achievements, awards and international affiliations of the school/university. The government's scheme of Mid Day Meal has received a noticeable response from poor children. The private sectors prepare their flyers, brochures or booklets to showcase their success. Some advertisements also motivate other kids by publishing picture of the toppers of the school/university. Some advertisements draw attention towards the scientific value of the product and some towards religion. Tourism also gets promoted through advertisements. Thus, advertisements touch almost all the sectors of human life. The huge applicability of advertisement in the business line makes it imperative to study the special features of an advertisement. These feature are basically divided into two categories: Format, Method and Mode.

Format of an Advertisement

1. **Attractive Design:** The advertisements are for attracting attentions of the consumers. An attractive design also speaks for the smart labour that goes in designing it. Some winter products show the landscape of cold countries and the ads of cold drinks are pictured in hot regions. The background scenery and the featured celebrity's photo-captured on glossy papers make an impactful appeal to the consumers.
2. **Colour:** Colour have language and the ad-designers use language of colours extensively. During Republic Day and Independence Day, we see that most of the advertisements use orange and saffron colours. The newspaper headlines also use orange, white and green – the tricolour as a sign of respect to the National Flag. The TV news and entertainment channels use these three colours in their logo and the subtitle strips.
3. **Language:** Language in the advertisement is convincing and persuasive. Some advertisements use simple and some use embellished language. Ornamental language is used for the high rate products and simple language is used for the advertisements with social message.

Method of an Advertisement

1. Consistency
2. Variations
3. Star Campaign
4. Brevity
5. Bias Free Language

Consistency

Achievement of target outcome becomes easy through the consistency in advertisements. The buyer today has excessive choice offers and in the plethora of advertisements, it is quite obvious to forget a product that is not advertised consistently. There should be an assertive and aggressive way of advertising.

Variations

Consistency is essential however repetition should be avoided. It is better to be consistent with content and not with presentation. There can be a series of the same advertisement with different pictures, people and presentation. Variation shows how the product covers the wider spectrum of public life.

Star Campaign

This is related to the credibility of the product. If a CEO of a company, a Director General of a University, a physician, lawyer or a doctor advertises, there is seen value addition and authenticity in the advertisement. The language in such advertisements is persuasive and piercing. The campaign of Swatch Bharat Abhiyan is spearheaded by the Super Star Amitabh Bachchan. In one of the advertisements, Akshay Kumar, the Hindi Cinema star gives a tagline, 'Satyagrah se Swachagrah tak' and associates the swachchata campaign with the historical Indian revolutionary movement led by the Father of the Nation of India.

Brevity

"Brevity is the soul of wit" says Francis Bacon, the 16th century British essayist. An advertisement selects words, phrases, idioms and other linguistic varieties that have potential richness to present the content in a nutshell. An advertisement is like a capsule that is tiny yet effective. The sentences should be clear and compact that can easily draw attention of people. Short sentences are easy to memorise. In some of the advertisements, some grammar rules are also not followed to make it compact and effective.

The advertisement for the cooked food service of Dominoz, the short tag line says, "I'm loving it" which has captured beyond limit attention of buyers.

Bias Free Language

Very recently we have seen the beauty product Fair and Lovely changing its name to Glow and Lovely. This is to remove any possibility of discriminatory policy and establish a unanimity across race, colour, caste and creed. An advertisement is a part of social communication and so it is expected to create an effective content that engages customers without any bias and stop any possible chain of the bandwagon effect in spreading discrimination. Discriminatory language is offensive and affective which should be avoided. Phrases like, Indians in the USA should be framed as Indian diaspora and a word likc 'Orientals' should be rephrased as 'Asians'. There can not be a rule book for the language of advertisement however linguistic ethicalities should be maintained to avoid any offensive remark that hurts the sentiments of any strata of human life.

Modes of Advertisement

1. Online Advertisement
2. Radio Advertisement
3. Print Media Advertisement
4. Crowdsourcing

Online Advertisement

Online advertisement is the most effective, convenient, facilitating and cost effective way for advertisement. Online shopping is a global market. Online shopping facilitates by offering end number of chances to explore the shopping sites by only scrolling and clicking. With the rising numbers of applications like Amazon Prime, Hotstar and Netflix and many gaming channels, even entertainment has become cheap in price and just a click away. This is because of the Audio Video presentation. Online advertisements cover a bigger demography of viewership and a vast spectrum of saleable goods that ranges from head to toe accessories, salons, medical shops, law firms and help agencies. Online advertisement has almost changed the way to communicate. It is a huge industry for employment as a 30 second ad needs a complete crew to shoot it. The status lines or tag lines used in these advertisements help create popularity and fan circles. Online platform also provide space for writing blogs. This further opens a gate for Content Development – a big world of words, imaginative skills blended with intellectual narration.

Radio Advertisement

In cities, Radio is treated as a secondary medium of information or entertainment. Nevertheless, Radio is an inseparable feature of a car. People listen to radio more with a purpose to get entertainment than to get information. In addition, the driving time may not be more than an hour a day. In absence of the visual effect, the advertisement is treated more as a diversion than as an information. In these circumstances, an advertisement remains unnoticed, howsoever wonderfully narrated it may be.

Print Media

Newspapers, magazines, brochures, pamphlets, flyers, leaflets etc. are the modes to advertise through print media. Print media advertisement receives followers only if the advertisement is not available on social media – online. In addition, generally the print media readership rate is also declining day in and day out. The general public prefers magazine for focused reading. The advertisement does not attract the reader unless it is either the only platform available or it fits into the choice criteria or it is uniquely designed, crafted or drafted. Some newspapers introduce a gift coupon scheme to attract the wider readership. Though newspapers are read more for the factual information than any hyperbolic and attractive status line of an advertisement.

Crowdsourcing

A public fair is the best place for crowdsourcing. A fair has an open market for all. The public does not come to a fair for shopping nevertheless almost everyone probably purchases one or the other thing. Now-a-days, crowdsource is one of the methods to attract and invite people to purchase as well as give suggestions to improve the product. Some also crowdsource near malls with offers to taste-and-buy schemes. The salespeople are politely persuasive and well behaved in crowdsourcing so as to remove any kind of embarrassment with the customer.

All in all, the advertisement is a strong weapon to persuade a customer. Advertisements are generally based on the observation skills and lessons learnt from the lived experiences. The language of an advertisement is conducive and easily comprehensive. Sometimes, advertisements are seen challenging other similar products. But it should not be humiliating to each other. An advertisement sometimes also spreads message of humour, love, affection and care for each other. The product in subject becomes a part of their success, achievement and happiness. Linguistic discipline, accuracy and crispness create the impact of effective communication through advertisements. Success in sale of a product owe much to the advertisements and for that originality is the key to make an appeal to the audience. The qualities of an advertisement can be summarised as:

1. Advertisements are to communicate a message
2. The communication style is user-friendly
3. The language is crisp and specific
4. The language must be free of any gender bias
5. Linguistic ethicalities should be strictly maintained
6. A genuine idea should be floated
7. Originality is irreplaceable
8. Common observation skills help create a meaningful message

Thus, an advertisement is a speaking and moving picture that informs, reminds, persuades, reinforces and thus makes all the assertive efforts to increase the saleability of the product.

Chapter - 5

Art of Negotiation

Negotiation: An Art

Negotiation is a type of communication that directly affects the speaker's image, prospect and career. Negotiation is an art that is associated more with the negotiator's mind than heart. It is to create a verbal web to win the expected favour from the communication in progress. It can be natural or acquired. Every single sentence in negotiation is spoken with the knowledge acquired from the past and the plans designed for the future. Negotiation is not a normal communication where a sender's message is decoded by the receiver and the feedback is dispatched. Negotiation is more about a deal, an agreement or a contract that is to be done at the outset of any formal communication. Any loose ended communication can severely affect the negotiation and the result of the same is to be stomached for times to come. A successful negotiation can lay the foundation for professional transparency and help establish a sustainable corporate relationship.

Negotiation is not limited only to trade and commerce. It is in fact an everyday affair. It is needed in personal as well as in professional circles. We can see negotiation between:

1. A landlord and a tenant
2. A shopkeeper and a customer
3. A fruit vendor and a customer

4. A domestic servant and the employer
5. A child and parent
6. An interior designer and the house/office owner
7. An applicant and a recruiter

Thus, negotiation is between a service provider and a service taker. Negotiation is basically a focused dialogue either between two companies, two parties or two individuals. Negotiation also needs consideration over the social and cultural aspects associated with the dialogue-executors. Negotiation is a sum total of sufficient knowledge, impressive communication skills and appropriate method and approach. These three features are the fundamental stones to negotiation. Knowledge helps beat fear, hesitation or doubt. Communication skills help arrange the logical arguments and appropriate method and approach makes the process of negotiation easy and target oriented and thus establish an image of smart and focused business man. These three features also have further sub-sets of intellectual action plans that aid formulate the negotiation roadmap. These subsets are identified as:

Knowledge

Knowledge of the financial support that is on hand and expected from any funding agency:

Knowledge of the estimated time and energy that is required for a successful negotiation.

Knowledge of the support system that is required in future in case negotiation is done successfully.

Knowledge of the mission and vision of the self and of the parties involved in negotiation.

Knowledge that negotiation is a kind of psychological process so a good state of mind and a critical thinking pattern is a prerequisite.

Knowledge that negotiation is creative as well as critical.

Knowledge that there needs to be a synergy between heart and head.

Communication Skills – Verbal and Non-verbal

The negotiator needs to be well versed with the language of communication.

The sentences being spoken need to be logically arranged.

The tone of speech needs to be polite and persuasive.

Any verbal clash must be avoided.

The negotiator needs to be brief as well as brilliant in demonstrating the arguments.

The language may be assertive but never aggressive.

Affirmative presentation, socialising attitude and formal dressing pave the way for successful negotiation.

The negotiator must be confident.

Confidence is derived from past experiences.

Confidence is a sign of awareness and agility.

Appropriate Method

It can be either inductive or deductive.

Inductive method starts with explaining the observations, discussing the monetary and non-monetary issues involved and thus presenting the concluding remarks.

Deductive method is to start with establishing the fact based conclusions first and then moving to citing a few example to substantiate the conclusions.

Thus, negotiation is not a casual conversation. It is highly technical and target centric communication. It is an art to deal. In case of unfavourable results of negotiation; the negotiator must not feel lost or defeated. Every skill has its own learning curve and every negotiator should keep a watch over the Professional Etiquettes that are prerequisites for successful negotiation.

Professional Negotiation Etiquettes

1. Self-evaluate the work method
2. See if a soft or a strict approach be developed

3. Self-regulate the work system
4. Be open to get feedback, oral or written
5. Scrutinise it neutrally and
6. Prepare a roadmap to smart negotiation

The art of negotiation is a test for effective communication. A smart negotiator believes in 'company first' approach. While making any sale related presentation, the negotiator would use a collective noun like "we" or the third person singular noun "my company". He may say,

1. We offer the best deal in …
2. We at so and so Company believe in building trust with our dealers and so….
3. As a proud employee at so and so Company I guarantee you of the bond of honesty and trust …
4. My company offers the best offer in the state …We facilitate our customers with all the essential services …
5. It is my privileged feeling to present before you the progress graph of the company of the last 5 years…

These sentences can create soft yet strong influence on the dealers. The negotiator shares the goodwill of the company and the bond of association that the employee shares with the company and thus makes positive and assertive influence over the dealers. Basically, the tone of courtesy, energetic presentation added with accurate knowledge help the negotiator to impress the opposite party and sign the deal in favour.

The negotiator's task is not limited only to showcase the company and the association in bright light. Sometimes, the negotiator's task is also challenged in times of adversity, conflict or any strong criticism against the company. At such crucial moments, a negotiator's ability to strategic communication (as discussed in the previous chapters) is tested. At the time of crisis, a negotiator needs to respond with more sincerity and diligence. The following suggestions may help to get control over any corporate storm:

1. Reminding the trust relation that is shared so far
2. Presenting the logical arguments with assertion and politeness
3. Presenting the review report that the company has produced to reinstate the lost trust
4. Being reasonable in giving account of the services provided
5. Being humble in accepting the services received
6. Being lawfully correct during self-defence and while laying allegations
7. Being extremely transparent in any financial matter
8. Being ethical to avoid any unprecedented threat or fear

Thus, a negotiator should act responsibly, keep an eye on company's image and the opponent's importance in the business deal.

There is a rough concept associate with negotiation that it incurs negative feelings and low credibility about the negotiator and the company. This concept is rough but not baseless. The credit for this goes to an immature negotiator who acts without realising the **Professional Negotiation Etiquette**. The immature negotiator might:

1. Enter into a verbal volley
2. Show desperation
3. Talk loose-ended
4. Speak with disrespect
5. Speak with under/over confidence
6. Behave insincerely
7. Carry insufficient information
8. Not be enthusiastic
9. Be incomprehensive
10. Underrate the importance of unity of time and place

The art of negotiation needs more attention in case of cross-cultural communication. Culture frames the ethnic identity that usually people protect and respect. A smallest verbal slip may affect the cultural emotions and that may become a reason for disrupted communication. A negotiator must take extra care to protect the cultural sentiments of all involved in the process of negotiation. People feel offended if their culture is misinterpreted or misquoted during any communication; personal or professional. To avoid any such unwanted embarrassment or derailed communication, a negotiator should use culture neutral language.

The art of negotiation is a journey that a negotiator makes from thought to action, perception to experience, dream to deal and abstract to concrete. Negotiation is not a simple conversation between two parties involved. It is strategic as well as structured. The parties involved have different aims and objectives. To convince the opposite party on the select terms and conditions is not easy. The market today is flooded with exciting and vibrant offers. The buyer has an easy access to switch from one to the other product. The negotiator's incompetency may lead towards conflict and inconclusive ending. The negotiation skills are meaningful as application not only as theory. If applied keenly, negotiation skills can build a strong relationship or otherwise it can destroy it.

Thus, the art of negotiation needs flexible attitude and strong arguments; constructive flow of thoughts and restrictive flow of anger and anxiety; and a descriptive contextual reference to the matter on hand without any mention of personal rivalry or rift. While framing the language of negotiation, the negotiator may use allegories and metaphors and make the optimum use of the interpersonal skills to create a favourable situation. Self-assessment, Self-confidence and Self-control are the prerequisites of the art of negotiation.

Self-assessment

Self-assessment is to:

Verify the truth about self-portrayal

Recognize the company's repute

Make use of indiscriminative language

Self-confidence

Self-confidence is to:

Speak with audible and clear voice

Dress up formally

Behave sophisticatedly

Be flawless in arguments

Self-control

Self-control is to be:

Assertive and not aggressive

Descent and not dramatic

Well researched and not evasive

With these three formative blocks a negotiator can build an impressive image of self and the company both. Such a negotiator easily overcomes the situation of any crisis, protects the brand name of the company and becomes a core link between the company of association and the other business groups.

Chapter - 6

Crisis Communication

It is quite unpleasant to note that crisis has ubiquitous presence. Though the good part is that crisis is not unmanageable; may it be a corporate climate or a social climate. In some cases, Crisis may hit without any prior notice whereas in some, crisis is anticipated, maybe as repercussion, after effect or consequence of past action. The presence of crisis can be seen from top management to the bottom line employee. It generates from opinion clashes to hatred to legal issues to image denting to discriminations to injuries and insults. Crisis has pervasive effect in the corporate climate. It hits silently and can make an irreparable damage if not controlled with strategic competence. Crisis is like a virus that remains unidentified and so gets success in spreading its impression to a larger circle. One needs to identify it through its characteristic impact that damages office system as well as office relations.

Crisis: A SWOT Analysis

Cri-sis, as the pronunciation implies, has power to make people *cry*. It is one such hurdle that remains hidden in the corporate climate and hits strongly, mostly without any notice of alarm. When crisis takes a full tangible form, the natural reaction of employees' is to curb it, to be victorious over it. Some take charge to reveal its real dark image and some also find it to be a monster and throw guards against it and accept their defeat. It is but obvious to forget that every crisis is unique in nature and appearance and so may not be perceptible at the pre-primary level. An unattended crisis can disrupt the repute and create a situation of threat and weakness of/for the company, the stakeholders and the staff. Contrary to this, if it is controlled and managed in time, the same crisis can pave the way and create an opportunity for the victims to emerge with more strength. It is imperative at this stage to make a SWOT analyse of Crisis. (Though SWOT analysis is highly recommended for Industry Analysis, here it is used to elaborate the word 'crisis' in the light of strength, weakness, opportunity and threat that is associated with it).

Crisis as Strength

Team work

An organisation comprises of team/teams of individuals who work together for a single goal. It is like choral singing and group dance where every individual sings and dances respectively in tune with the orchestra. The spirit of a team is tested best during the time of crisis. The organisational team must work with synchrony and synergy to fight against crisis. Their collective efforts and positive attitude create moral support system that encourages all to manage crisis on hand. These team workers respect each other's differences – socio-cultural, linguistic or even ideological. A mature team works with fresh mind, make an intellectual exchange of ideas, develop a bond of faith and work hard during the time of crisis. For such indulgent and sincere team, crisis can be transformed into a reason to emerge stronger in the corporate climate.

Intuitive knowledge

"If you see clouds going crosswind, there is a storm in the air." This proverbial statement speaks volumes about reading the signals before any incident takes place. Intuitive knowledge is the ability to understand the situation and internally sense its intensity and imminent danger. Crisis needs to be identified when it is in its tiniest form. If it is attended with utter priority and sincerity, crisis can be managed at an early stage. Intuitive knowledge can be inherent or acquired through experience.

Able leadership

Crisis also creates chance to sharpen leadership skills. A leader works at multiple fronts. A leader works with strategic mind, employs all the essentialities of effective leadership, keeps focused vision and works diligently. Such leaders pass through the tests of experience, patience, diligence, coherence and resilience. The leader's language in the time of crisis plays major role in controlling it. A leader, without linguistic discipline not only declines from the position but also creates another crisis for the company as well as for self.

Contingency plan

Contingency is any abrupt and sudden emergency at a departmental level that can dismantle the company's repute in one blow. In case of mismanagement of data, contingency is an unprecedented havoc that can create an upside down situation for all. It is highly advisable to procure tools and techniques that can be useful to meet with any contingency. Contingency can be seen from matter of sudden data loss to a life taking accident in organisation. Contingency can be handled with previously prepared and procured backup plans and safety measures respectively. It is said that precaution is better than cure. As a precautionary measure, a contingency plan needs to be designed to act quickly with accuracy. Such a backup plan helps avoid or at least reduce the impact factor of the contingency.

Crisis as Weakness

Procrastination

Procrastination is a sign of lethargic behaviour which is not accepted even in normal situation. Lethargic behaviour during crisis is like inviting individual as well as collective doom at/of an organisation. The habit of delaying pollutes work culture and work structure. A lethargic person behaves like a zombie and uses uninspiring and dull language that creates a spiral of negativity in the organisation. During the time of crisis, it is expected to work ahead of time. Procrastination makes the situation more critical and grave.

Lack of communication

The message flow in the organisation can be upward or downward; horizontal or lateral. May it be any, but it needs to be followed with more attentiveness during the time of crisis. When this flow gets disrupted due to any personal or technical problem, crisis enforces strong foothold over situation and further worsens the situation.

Poor leadership

Leadership is an all-inclusive term. A leader who divides and rule, disseminates work injudiciously, expects without self-involvement or lags behind in taking ownership during the times of adversities is a poor leader. A poor leader is that inadequate captain whose poor navigation and steering abilities become the reason for the organisation/steamer to sink. Crisis needs to be handled creatively and critically. A leader's role becomes more crucial during this unforeseen situation. A leader's poor network with fellow workers or egocentric behaviour can bring fatal results for the organisation.

Crisis as Opportunity

To be innovative

Some employees know the art to transform any pain into gain. They are recognised as game changers or trend setters. They know the skill to take the untrodden road and craft their roadmap during the time of crisis. For such corporate employees, crisis brings in opportunity to act with more critical and innovative measure. Their logical reasoning and diligent work ability become their guiding force.

To be calm and humorous

Humour works as psychological immunity to fight against any crisis. It is quite obvious to feel disturbed in the time of crisis. However, an intellectual employee remains calm, unaffected and balanced and use humour or lighter fun sentences to reduce the impact factor of crisis. Humour helps balance the levels of anxiety and anger and gives a newer perspective to deal with crisis.

Manage emotions

A potential worker knows the importance of emotional management and how to take right decisions at right times. Impulsive decisions may drive in more disturbing factors that increase the intensity of crisis. An organisation needs employees who are practical and meticulous in their actions and behaviour. Emotional or sensitive behaviour may influence actions or decisions and may derail the whole planned flow of action. One who can strike balance between emotional fluctuations, can convert crisis into opportunity.

Realisation of self-importance

To be aware of self-importance is to be aware of the expectation that the organisational duties have from the employees. This awareness should not lead any employee towards arrogance. They should demarcate the lines between arrogance and self-importance. Employees and leaders should know the worth of their presence and active participation during the time of crisis. There needs to be shared responsibility among employees to fight against the adverse situations of crisis.

Crisis as Threat

Nervous behaviour

Last but not the least is to foresee threat in crisis. It is quite obvious to get nervous while facing anything unprecedented and unfamiliar. Crisis hits in newer forms with newer challenges and risk factors. It is but obvious to loose courage and develop feelings of fear and insecurity. With such fragile psychological status, an employee/

leader feels threatened. Such a person gets surrounded by the thoughts loss and defeat. Nervousness makes person unnecessarily defensive.

Lack of confidence

Threat takes away confidence and positive energy. A threatened person works under pressure and develops feelings of surrender. Such a person loses confidence in self as well as in colleagues. Crisis needs extra care and attention and if a person is buckled under pressure of threat and loses confidence and courage; the work efficiency gets damaged.

Lack of trust

This is another offshoot of threat that develops other sinking feelings of loss of trust within self and among colleagues. Suspicion and doubt dwell where trust is lacking. Trust issues jeopardise the cords of relationship. To handle crisis dexterously, one needs to disseminate work among colleagues and in absence of trust, the dissemination goes haywire. It is important to put trust in colleagues for smooth action. Lack of trust or mistrust exhilarates the intensity of threat and terror. Consequently, there are seen high possibilities of emotional outburst due to anxiety, anger and self-doubt.

This SWOT analysis of crisis shows that crisis can be unprecedented and consequential. However, balanced and practical perception and adequate preparation are the major tools that help tame the intensity of crisis. The situation of crisis itself is vulnerable and fragile. Crisis also has psychological impact over work efficiency. It depends on an employee's agility and ability whether a person fights, frights or flights against/of/from crisis. Language precision and influential communicative skills play major role in managing crisis. The following figure shows the multifaceted role of linguistic precision that helps control organisational crisis. The communicator should speak:

1. Empathetically
2. Confidently

3. Practically
4. Strategically
5. Analytically
6. Decisively
7. Encouragingly
8. Emphatically
9. Frankly
10. Humorously
11. Non-prejudicially
12. Non-discriminatingly

A unique thing about crisis is that it is omnipresent and ever-changing. Every crisis requires a set of different tools and techniques to deal with it. It is not easy to figure out the severity of crisis at the outset. It has a situational flow. At the primary stage of crisis, it is difficult to predict whether crisis will affect an individual or a group of employees. It can be either a tip of an iceberg that appears small in size but is heavier and dangerous in its actual form or it can be just a bubble of fear that is big in size and bursts only at a tiny prick. May the case of crisis be any, the organisation cannot weigh it light and commit mistake of ignoring it by developing ostrich policy. The abruptly erupted crisis leave employees awestruck and restless. In addition, the flood of news and rumours attack the individual and affect the workability of the employees. In such situation, the employees' ability to think, plan and act is challenged. Not only that, there are high chances for complications and confusions and consequently crisis takes strong foothold. Any tiny mistake can become the reason for organisational damage or decline. It is thus necessary to stay prepared to fight against any unprecedented crisis. In short, the organisation should prepare for the worst and hope for the best.

Types of Crisis

There are various types of crisis and every crisis brings in hazardous situation. Majorly, the types of crisis are noticed to be:

1. Legal Crisis
2. Financial Crisis
3. Accidental Crisis
4. Behavioural Crisis
5. Ethical Crisis

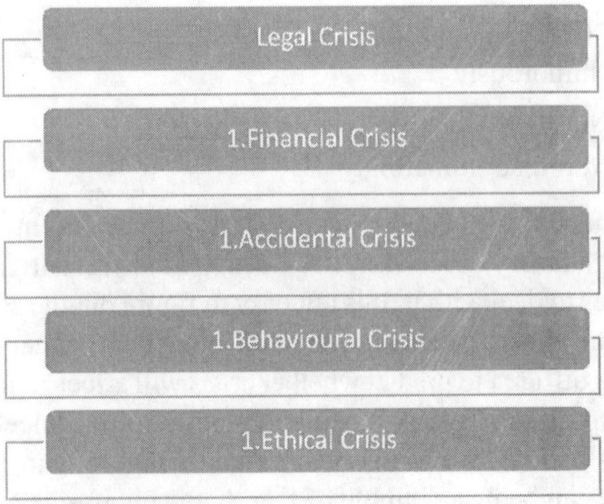

Source: Authors' representation.

Figure 11: Major types of crisis.

Legal Crisis

The success of an organisation depends on its strong or weak networking with other organisations that either supply resources or purchase the product. In any of such give and take, or in a smallest case of deception, breach of contract or false allegations, one organisation can sue the other. There can be cases of fraud, bribery or supplying damaged goods or also cases of discriminations, boycott, harassment or irregular payment of salary. Such legal crisis need intervention of organisational lawyers who investigate into the matter and bring to the floor the truth. To meet with the legal crisis, organisations should appoint a lawyer who acts as legal advisor and also appears in court when needed.

Financial Crisis

Finance is the spinal code of an organisation. Any case of fraud or bankruptcy can damage an organisation's financial strength as well as goodwill and repute. There must be financial investment of other parties in the organisation which gets badly affected when stock market crashes. In case of bank lending, the issue may take a form of legal case. It takes no time for an organisation to collapse. Such situations are beyond repair. To avoid such distressful situation, an organisation must spend according to the yearly budget prepared by the experts. It is also necessary to know that the organisation may be lender but never a borrower. On time payment of all the due bills and making proper scrutiny of monthly bills can help the organisation keeping track of the collective expenditure of the organisation. The employees should remember that the goodwill of their organisation should always be protected.

Accidental Crisis

Accidental crisis ranges from data loss to human loss on organisation. Such situations leave the employees stunned and speechless. The employees may not be able to stop any such disastrous accidents but their proactive behaviour can at least reduce the deadly impact of it. As data saved hard drive or google drive can compensate the data loss; similarly Life Insurance policies of employees can also compensate an accidental human loss.

Behavioural Crisis

This kind of crisis appear small in size and never a matter of open discussion, however its effect cannot go unnoticed. It can be on horizontal line or vertical line of employees. The arrogant or angry leader, the disobedient employee, a gossip lover or a nontechnical colleague and their typical behavioural patterns are difficult to be managed. Some employees are always late and some leave early without completing their work. Some are spoilers who neither work not allow others to work. Some angry leaders use foul and abusive language and some subordinates lack general decency in language.

The discriminatory behaviour also affects work culture. Such organisation becomes a rotten place where work efficiency, collective productivity, interpersonal connectivity, general rapport among colleagues and motivation to work are badly affected. Trust issues and non-reliance among employees is a general problem who all escape from taking ownership and blame each other. Such organisation works utterly unprofessionally and so their growth chart remains un-updated.

Ethical Crisis

The present day corporate climate is multi-cultural, multi-talented and multi-dimensional. If the employees behave unprofessionally (as discussed in Behavioural Crisis), the fall is imminent. To keep any ethical crisis at bay, some disciplinary parameters should be set and be followed willingly. To maintain ethical cord of conduct, it is extremely important for every employee to be morally own their duties and responsibilities. Such an organisation grows in no times. Ethical behaviour is about encouraging a colleague, keeping transparency in office matters, following hard work over an easy path of appeasement. The leader should keep transparency in case of downward communications. A leader should not develop a selective approach. Groupism and favouritism should be avoided strictly. In otherwise case, employees feel isolated from mainstream system and they feel demotivated to work. There should be a formal introduction of a new entrant at the general meetings. This will encourage an energetic and enthusiastic involvement of the new entrant in the organisation. It will also help establish cordial relation among all employees. The warm and healthy relation among employees adds energy to the efficiency. The ambience should be gender neutral and so any case of harassment or bullying may be terminated at a very primary level. The employees should remain loyal and committed to their work and the leaders should make them feel motivated to work for the organisation. Some smaller yet important actions should be taken by the leaders. During festivals like Diwali, sweets should be distributed by the leaders as a sign of greeting.

To manage with crisis, a proactive and proficient communication team should be arranged. Crisis management is a two-end process of planning and execution. Communication is a connecting link between these two ends. In case of delayed communication or complicated communication, planning remains unexecuted or misexecuted. To avoid any such complexity, an organisation should form a group or committee that effectively co-ordinates to carry out the plan successfully. This committee comprises of executives who:

1. Identify crisis
2. Plan the operational flow
3. Execute the plan
4. Coordinate with planners and executors
5. Follow instructions and work as ordered
6. Evaluate and provide feedback

These six committees remain in common contact with each other. This is necessary to keep tracks of the progress of the plan. Crisis emerge suddenly but its management plan needs to be designed beforehand. Planning and work dissemination are time consuming activities. Nevertheless, these activities should be imperatively formed to avoid any long term damage. Such plans will reduce the long term harm at the organisation. There should be personal involvement of the leaders or the senior executives who advise, guide or direct the committee to plan and work in the right direction. Some organisations, as a part of their public concern, arrange press conference and also allow media houses to take in-depth interview. This is to openly share their crisis management skills. Such organisations appoint spokespersons who prepare press notes and communicate on behalf of the organisation. They are also accountable to portray the true and inspiring success story of the organisation's crisis management. By maintaining such professional standards, the organisations show their responsibility to be loyal to public interest and emotions. Such communication strategies help an organisation to live up to their brand name and earn public trust.

Chapter - 7

LSRW: The Essential Skill Set

There is no doubt that communication is an essential set of soft skills. Unfortunately, in many schools and technical degree colleges and universities, these skills are side-lined under the shadow of technical curriculum. These four essential skills are Listening, Speaking, Reading, and Writing. A very common process of communication describes how a message is sent (encoded) and received (decoded) by the reader. Thus, listening and reading are receiving activities while speaking and writing are transmitting activities.

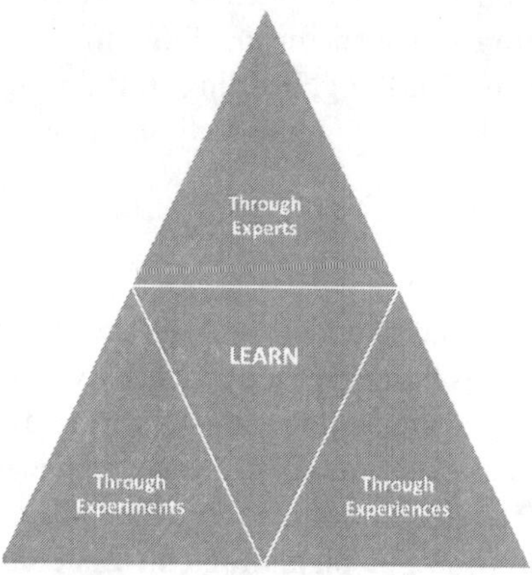

Source: authors' presentation.

Figure 12: Three Es of Learning.

Some successful people are born with the required communication skills and some develop through learning that can be acquired through three 'E's.

First, we learn from experts. These experts may be our parents or teachers from our childhood or colleagues or mentors at workplace. Secondly, we learn through our experiences. As it has been said, 'experience is the best teacher'. Sometimes, we learn through the experience of our near ones. We will not commit the mistakes that they might have committed and we will surely follow them if they are rewarded for their actions. And the third learning is gained from experiments. This is where we test our inherent as well as acquired abilities. This is more a pragmatic stage than a theoretic one. We observe our choice of words and the tone with which we speak with our colleagues. We see the impact of our words and tone. Accordingly we develop our communication skills. We also bring change in our dressing style and behaviour pattern when we realise that change is the need of the hour. Nobody wants to stay outdated. To be in tune with the world around, we all apply new knowledge systems and learn by adopting the experimented truths.

Learning should be revised at times. Learning in communication is more concrete when practiced in daily life. The world of communication is based on the four infrastructural pillars namely – Listening, Speaking, Reading and Writing. These pillars are the essential skills of communication. They are discussed in the following sections:

Listening

The first thing we need to understand (by the way, understanding requires listening!) is the difference between *listening* and *hearing*. Of course, listening is impossible without hearing. To cure difficulty in hearing, there are hearing aid or hearing devices invented but there is no aid or device invented to cure listening difficulties. The reason is listening is not physiological. Listening is a mental process. Ears take care of hearing while listening is taken care of by mind. We can avoid a sight by closing our eyes but we cannot avoid sounds without making conscious efforts. Hearing is the ability to perceive various sounds. This is a natural process. Once the sounds are perceived, the mind bifurcates the sounds into two categories; familiar sound and unfamiliar sound. The mind also helps to understand whether we want to pay attention to the sound signals or not. The moment we decide to pay attention to the sounds detected through the vibration of the ears, hearing gets transformed into listening. In case we find the sound signals as unimportant or disturbing, we stop paying any attention and we discard those sounds and identify them as Noises. Hearing is just the messenger's task. On the other hand, listening begins when ears complete their task. Listening is processing, not just passing the audio. Interestingly, there can be hearing without listening but there can't be listening without hearing. We hear the sounds and listen to people. Listening to people is totally different process from listening to devices. We deal with people and control devices. Listening to people involves thinking, feeling, reacting, and acting.

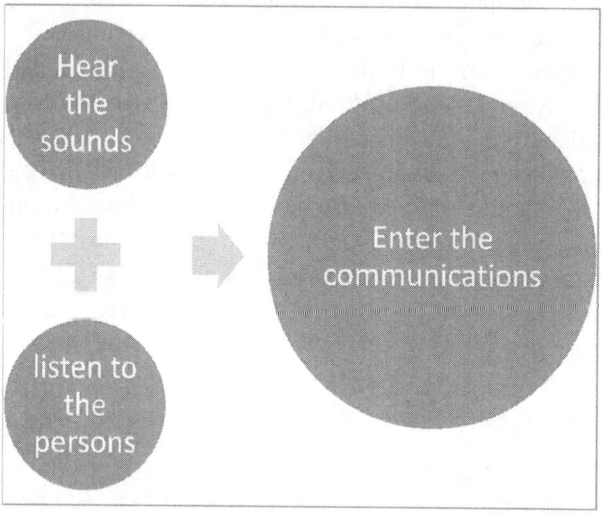

Source: Authors' presentation.

Figure 13: Listening, Hearing and Communication.

The listening process is a comprehensive one. Listening happens in brain, not only in ears. We like certain voices while dislike noises. We prefer to listen to some people while avoid others. Sometimes, we want that other listen to us while other times, we prefer to listen. Hearing happens in auto mode while listening requires training – formal or informal.

From the smaller unit like family to the larger unit like society and the universe, we have been actively and passively, directly and indirectly learning the importance of listening attentively. Though in certain cultures, hierarchy decides who listens to whom and how much. When we reach the stage where we need to work in teams with organization(s) to make a living, we tend to forget listening lessons and start judging. This may put us in trouble, if we do not accept soon that listening is a skill. Communicating with colleagues is more formal compared to communicating with friends, family, neighbours, or classmates.

Listening is a skill, which we can either develop from scratch or polish it from its existing level. One must accept that one's formal education or work experience does not merely guarantee development of listening skill. Skills can be acquired, adopted and developed on the basis of our experience and knowledge. Today's dynamic corporate culture and branches of domain knowledge expect the employees to be equipped with soft skills; and communication skills is the much sought after skill in corporate world. We should not limitedly understand communication skills as fluency, vocabulary, or accent only. The most important communication skills are listening. Not because very few people have these skills now a days but because listening is receiving, not spending only. When we listen, we receive attention, information,

Source: Authors' presentation.

Figure 14: Categorisation of Listening Skill.

knowledge, ideas, and instruction. Listening is gathering all of these, which helps us very often.

If one has not received formal and informal listening training (through parents, teachers and trainers) in right extent at right time, there are chances to get baffled and feel lost and ask questions like "*Why should I listen to that person?*" Until we are convinced with this why factor, we will not know how we should listen. Not to listen can be perceived as ego or ignorance. We must use our listening skills all the time irrespective of we are supposed to listen or not because there is no loss in listening. There may be many times big loss in not listening though. We might not only miss important information by not cultivating habit of listening but also miss opportunities. To grow in the corporate world, one must keep one's eyes and ears open all the time.

Everyone does not have the same amount of ability and readiness to listen. It is believed that compared to extroverts, introverts listen more intently (Taylor, 2020; Remund, 2015). Putting the debate about the personality types in corporate world aside, let us assume one is ready for listening. When one has answer(s) of the question '*why should I listen?*', one gets ready to be involved in communication process. One's readiness to begin the conversation does not assure that one will be involved in the communication process till end. To carry on listening is difficult, especially when communication is not pleasant or not as expected. Listening becomes pretended or acted when the listener wants to end the unwanted communication. At workplace, most of the time unwanted communications don't end without wasting time and energy because the listener is not able or willing to say, '*I don't want to listen to this.*' or '*Let's end the communication here for now.*' The compulsion to carry on the listening (out of courtesy or respect), especially from the superiors or customers produces useless conversations. But the listeners are convinced somehow that they need to listen, the fake listening keeps going on. When listeners are attentive and are willingly ready to listen to others; listening becomes fruitful. Their listening expressions make others feel that they are listening attentively. First sign is body language.

Pretending to listen or listening passively is not as bad as not listening. Listening actively is better than passive listening. One must carefully select the best option among (1) no listening, (2) passive listening, and (3) active listening.

Table 1: Listening Types and Reasons

Listening types	*Readiness*	*Ability*	*Mental presence*	*Self-interest*
No listening	X	x	x	x
Passive listening	✓	✓	X	x
Active listening	✓	✓	✓	✓

Source: Authors' presentation.

We can understand these three listening types with reference to readiness to listen, ability to listen, mental presence, and self-interest:

Readiness to listen can be spontaneous or a part of reflex action unless one decides not to listen.

Ability to listen can be related to more than just physical listening ability. One may be ready to listen to but may not be able to (reasons explained later).

In some situations we observe our colleagues or experience ourselves lacking **mental presence** or the absent mindedness.

Table 2: Examples of Listening Types and Reasons

Listening types	*Readiness to listen*	*Ability to listen*	*Mental presence*	*Self-interest*
No listening	Ego clash among colleagues	Work overload	Death in a family	Discontinued rules and regulations
Passive listening	✓	✓	Late for home	10-year plan
Active listening	✓	✓	✓	✓

Source: Authors' presentation.

Self-interest is the answer to the question – *How am I going to be benefited by being a part of this listening? What is there for me in this conversation?* - Self-interest is external unlike the above three.

Listening Types

We can bifurcate the listening in three types as:

Absence of listening: One's expressed or unexpressed unwillingness to listen to others can be because of lack of all four reasons mentioned in the table above.

Let us see the examples:

- When one has issues of ego clashes with one's colleague, one would not be ready to listen to the colleague besides one is able to listen, mentally present, and the presence of possible self-interest in that colleague's conversation.
- In case of work overload, one would be compelled to avoid or postpone the communication despite readiness. This is lack of ability to listen.
- In worst circumstances such as a death in a family, one may have both – readiness and ability to listen to but one knows that one would be able to hear all conversation but not able to listen to any.
- When a colleague is going to describe how irrelevant the rules and regulations in the organisation were, which are now replaced with the new ones; one would not care to listen as those are not applicable to one now. Self-interest is the listeners' judgment about what is their (personal benefit) in conversations.

Passive listening

Passive listening occurs when the listeners just want to hear but do not want to take the conversations seriously or do not want to act upon the conversation once it is completed. The listener would have readiness and ability to listen but not mental presence or self-interest.

Examples:

- The subordinates are getting late for home and when they are about to leave their office, the superior walks to them and starts instructing. The subordinates would not prefer not to listen (mainly due to hierarchy). So, they just nod their heads in pretention. They are mentally at home.
- The contractual employees' contract is over and they have been given termination notice. They are asked to all-staff meeting about next 10-year plan of their organisation. The employees don't see what is in that meeting for them.

Active listening: Active listening is the situation of presence of readiness to listen, willingness to listen, self-interest, and no absent mindedness among the listeners. Generally, if the fourth factor i.e., self-interest is present, the remaining three appears without efforts.

Examples:

- The H.R. manager has called you to discuss your performance appraisal.

We need to understand that rather grouping people in the categories of not a listener, passive listener, and active listener; we need to group listening itself in these categories. In other words, these listening types are not personality or person specific, the types are situational. An employee may change role, from time to time, among all four types.

Transition from No Listening to Active Listening

Of course, no listening is worst and active listening is the best way of listening. One needs to be aware of what one practices most at the workplace – no listening, passive listening, or active listening. Some of us know what types of listening we are habituated to while some of us may not be aware about this. Some of us know what types of listening we follow on certain occasions (e.g., during meetings) only. Sometimes we clarify with our colleagues whether we have listened right or not. Some corporate houses have mentorship programs, where they train the employees in developing their communication skills. A lot about us at workplace is known to others but invisible to us. We may not be the right judge for ourselves and our skills.

Johari window is a good model or technique developed by the psychologists Joseph and Harrington. This is often used technique in corporate training and mentorship. The technique is presented with combination of four quadrants known as Johari Window. The quadrants are called Arena, Blind spot, Façade, and Unknown. Arena represents things about ourselves, which are known to us as well as others (e.g., our position in an organization). Blind spot represents things unknown to us but known to others (e.g., how fast we speak). Façade represents things we know about ourselves but others are not aware about it (e.g., personal matters). Unknown represents things about ourselves known neither to ourselves nor to others (e.g., how will we react when provoked).

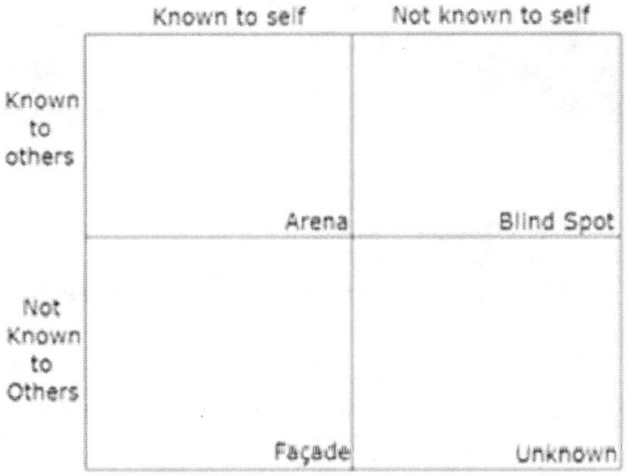

Source: Adapted from Johari Window model.

Figure 15: Relating listening to JoHari Window.

Ask your colleagues or mentors –*Do I listen actively?* No need to categorise ourselves by asking *Am I an active listener?* If your colleagues or mentors are frank and helpful, they would give you honest answer. This demands one more set of skills i.e., how to ask for help for self-improvement, who to ask, and how to react when the help is offered.

When you request your colleagues or mentors to judge your listening type, most probably they would say 'most of the time' or 'sometimes' or simply 'yes' to cut it short. Thank them for their help and think about their answers. If the feedback says you listen actively, you need to maintain your readiness, ability, presence of mind, and self-interest. If the feedback is that you tend to listen passively, it is a relief that you do listen at least most of time but you need to remove complacency and strive to improve for active listening. If the feedback is *you avoid listening most of the time*, you need to accept it first and then look at the two ways to practice active listening as shown in Fig. (1) From A to B and then from B to C. (2) From A to C directly.

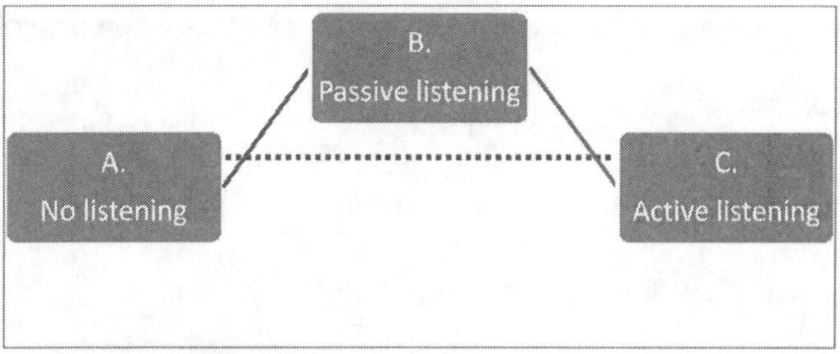

Source: Authors' representation.

Figure 16: Two ways to practice active listening.

It is relatively longer process to traverse to active listening directly from no listening (A to C), compared to go over via passive listening (A to B, then B to C). But in order to take the route via B, one must not practice passive listening intentionally. Meaning, if one can jump over passive listening, one must without worrying about first practicing passive listening. The key to make transition towards active listening is to develop readiness and ability to listen first and then work on mental presence and self-interest.

Once we achieve the state of active listening, we must thrive to remain in the state till we work in the corporate no matter how big and frequent the distractions arrive. We must regularly take feedback about our listening skills and listening type and keep improving it.

Listening Culture

Fortunately (for superiors) and unfortunately (for subordinates) organisations still follow the hierarchy culture, where those who are in power expect from those who are expected to obey them. There are corporates which are keen to listen to the frontline and middle level employees though. Only those who work there know about the presence or absence of listening culture in their organisation. Very few would publicly and openly discuss about who listens to whom in their organisation due to policy, work culture or fear. Since decades businesses talk about democratic organisations and democratic leadership but actual practice cannot be measured accurately. For example, those who talk to customers (frontline staff and dealers/retail distributors) would know more about customers and market compared to superiors seating in ivory towers and expecting their people to listen to them. It is sad that asking questions in a part of corporate world is sometimes considered as not listening. 'Just listen, don't ask questions' is a toxic culture in some corporate houses. Listening must not be confused with taking orders or instructions. Leaders can either create a listening culture in their organisations or wait for their employees to spread negative word of mouth about lack of listening culture in their organisation. The latter option may create obstacle in front of leaders in attracting creative and talented people to their organisation.

Leaders get ideas from listening to their followers not by making them listen.

When the listening culture is introduced and practiced in organisations, it is possible that employees, especially newly recruited ones, would hesitate to open up and talk. Organisation may miss the important inputs and listening from these employees, if they work under the impression that like at most of the corporates, they are there to just listen. In this situation, superiors can assure the employees that they will be listened to.

There are four ways leaders can develop the listening culture in organisations:

1. **Send agenda before hand:** Not only before meeting but before every conversation, if the employees know what that conversation is going to be about, they get chance to speak and organisations get an opportunity to listen to them. Organisation's calling the staff members for a meeting like a coach gathers the football team members to pray before the match does not make sense. Sending agenda for meetings to the participants beforehand is practiced in good corporates. If it is not a proper meeting but a short announcement, still the participants must know what it is going to be about so that they can prepare to participate. Superiors' calling subordinates over intercom to come to their office makes subordinates wonder what it is it going to be about till the subordinates reaches the superiors' office. The subordinates must get time to think and collect information about the matter of the conversation.
2. **Eliminate Head of the Table System:** In the *Head of the Table* tradition, the seniormost person or head in the hierarchy occupies the central chair of the table and the people junior to the head flank on the sides. This arrangement looks nice at family dinner but there is no relevance of it in 21st century corporate meetings and presentations, except showing royal-like power! It is worse than prisoners in prison share-passing (sharing thoughts one by one) seating in a circular arrangement. When seated in a circular seating arrangement, everyone (irrespective of hierarchy) can listen to one another. The circular seating makes the superior look one of the subordinates.

3. **Ask and Encourage:** Superiors must not hesitate to ask even silly questions if they feel others are hesitated to speak. Asking and sharing of questions, suggestions, advices, opinions, views, etc. not only encourages employees to participate but also gives them feeling that someone wants to listen to them. Leaders must not wait for the employees to say, 'If I may…', 'If you ask me…', 'May I say something?'
4. **Short meetings:** Finally, the longer the conversations, presentations, and meetings; more likely it is for the participants to lose interest in communication. One must speak less in order to listen more. Three meetings of twenty minutes each are better than one meeting of an hour. The meetings must not end by one person speaking alone and others waiting to get listened to.

Listening Manners and Etiquettes

There are sets of manners and etiquettes, which help the employees to stay and grow in corporate environment. While very common manner is to look into the eyes of the person who is speaking while listening to but it is not welcome in all cultures. For example, while talking to counterparts from country such as Japan, it is considered as bad manner to look into someone's eyes while communicating. In some countries, it is believed that if you are not nodding your head while listening means you are not understanding the conversation.

Notes

One should not try to frown to show seriousness, smile too much or laugh too much to show that one is attentively listening to the one who is speaking. Rather using body language, one should take notes of what one is listening to. By taking notes, we do not mean writing all the time in a diary or notepad. One can take mental notes too. One way to take mental note is to revise and reflex upon the communication just happened. Later, when a pen and a paper are handy and if necessary, one can download the mental notes onto paper.

Patience

Listening skill is also judged by one's patience to let the speaker finish the speaker's long conversation. At times, we get impatient to listen to long sentences and information overload and we tend to interrupt so that the speaker cut it short. This may occur when we are in hurry but cannot avoid conversation. Asking 'Can I come back to you later?' is the solution to this situation. Hurried listening is worse than postponed listening.

'Beg your pardon'

A mistake we often commit while listening is guessing when we do not understand direct meaning, hidden meaning, or hint in the conversation. The reasons for our opting for guessing could be either fear of asking to clarify or lack of knowledge as to how to ask for clarification, especially from superiors. It is not impoliteness to ask superiors to clarify if subordinates do not get clarity over the point of discussion. Guessing, instead of asking to repeat, leads to miscommunication.

Confirmation

We often hear the listeners using phrases such as 'understood', 'got it', 'got the point', etc. during or after conversations. Confirmations give signals to the one who is speaking that the listener has received the message and meaning of the communication. Confirmation must not be mechanical or pretended to satisfy the speakers' ego or to give speakers false assurance that someone is listening to them.

Listening to Translated Communication

One of the challenges in listening is listening and interpreting translated communications. In multi-national diverse corporate settings, translation is not limited to languages only. In addition to translation of languages, communications in corporate it includes translation of culture and technology (mode of communications) also.

Cultural Translation

Imagine communication of two employees – A and B working in a multinational company. A is born and brought up in India by Indian family while B in the U.S. by an American family. Both can speak (and comprehend) English language. Besides both of them speaking a common language, both may not listen to and comprehend each other in every communication. Communication gap may arise due to cultural difference. For example, employee A would listen to multiple uses of American slangs and workplace jargons, which may confuse A but would be very common for B.

Mode-Based Translation

We do not listen to the spoken words only. We listen through modern multimedia and internet. This leads to alternative of communicating synchronous (face to face online) or asynchronous (recorded) or mix of both (blended). The listening may fail or become less effective due to such reasons as issue with devices and/or connectivity. Listening to mode-based translated communications may include challenges of cultural differences too.

Listening Between the Lines

We have heard and read a lot about *reading between the lines*. We also need to develop a skill to 'listen between the lines'. The sugar-coated words spoken softly can have thundering meanings. For example, "You better listen to me." means 'Don't argue. I don't want to listen to you.', 'We have high expectations from you.' means be prepared for walking extra miles. 'One needs to justify one's salary.' means your output is not up to the mark. There are very limited works available on 'listening between the lines'; as summarised below:

Table 3. Year-wise entries for keywords "listening between the lines" on Google Scholar

Sl.No.	*Year*	*References*
1.	2019	Tigunova, Anna, et al. "Listening between the lines: Learning personal attributes from conversations." *The World Wide Web Conference*
2.	2019	Kale, Verna. "Listening between the Lines:" Hills Like "White Elephants" and "A Clean, Well-Lighted Place".
3.	2019	Neubert, Nils. "Reading and Listening Between the Lines: Ideas on Singing the Short and Open Vowels [I],[...], and [Y], and the Long and Closed Vowels [e...],[o...], and [ø...] in German." *Journal of Singing* 75.5: 567-570.
4.	2016	Gasper, Giles, Tom McLeish, and Hannah E. Smithson. "Listening between the lines: medieval and modern science." *Palgrave Communications* 2.1: 1-11.
5.	2014	Hudson, Andrew Sinclair. "Pentecostal History, Imagination, and Listening between the Lines: Historiographic Creativity for Writing Histories of the Marginalised." *Pneuma* 36.1: 25-44.
6.	2012	Fraser, Catriona, and Barbara F. Kelly. "Listening between the lines: Social assumptions around foreign accents." *Australian Review of Applied Linguistics* 35.1: 74-93.
7.	2010	Simpkins, Maureen A. "Listening between the Lines: Reflections on Listening, Interpreting and Collaborating with Aboriginal Communities in Canada." *The Canadian Journal of Native Studies* 30.2: 315.
8.	2008	Crowley, Kelley. "Listening Between the Lines: A Rhetorical Analysis of Conservative Talk Radio."
9.	2006	Corso, Stephine. "Listening Between the Lines: Understanding Jean-Marie Le Pen's Public Discourse on Unemployment."
10.	2004	Campbell, Nick. "Listening between the lines: a study of paralinguistic information carried by tone-of-voice." *International Symposium on Tonal Aspects of Languages: With Emphasis on Tone Languages*.
11.	2003	Muggli, M. E., and R. D. Hurt. "Listening between the lines: what BAT really thinks of its consumers in the developing world." *Tobacco control* 12.1: 104-104.
12.	2001	Smith, Anna Deavere. *Talk to me: Listening between the lines*. Random House
13.	1998	Pinker, Steven. "Listening between the lines."
14.	1970	Spence, Donald P., and Barry Grief. "An experimental study of listening between the lines." *The Journal of nervous and mental disease* 151.3: 179-186.

Source: https://scholar.google.com/scholar?as_vis=1&q=allintitle:+%22Listening+between+the+lines%22&hl=en&as_sdt=1,5 [Accessed 10 Feb 2021]

Listening exercises

1. Make a list of who all you listened to today. What did you listen? Why did you listen to them?
2. List out how many people listened to you today? Why? What was it about?
3. Describe, as a child, what did you like to listen to the most?
4. Describe, as a child, who did you like to listen to the most? Why?
5. Note down the conversation where you did not have readiness to listen to it.
6. Note down the conversation where you did not have ability to listen to it.
7. Note down the conversation where you did not have mental presence in it.
8. Note down the conversation where you did not have self-interest in it.
9. Narrate the conversation you do not like to listen to.

Speaking

Unlike in case of unwanted hearing, where one needs to make efforts (like covering ears) to avoid it, speaking is voluntary. Unlike sounds fall on our ears almost all the time, words do not come out unwanted. Speaking is not only voluntary or deliberate but also effort driven. One can pretend not to have listen to but cannot pretend not to have spoken. Listening is receiving while speaking is expressing.

All children don't begin speaking at the same age. Since birth, our abilities to hear and to speak work differently. For example, imparting speaking ability in a child born with hearing loss is different from imparting hearing ability in a child born mute. Thanks to hearing aid available for infants; a child can learn speaking at very early age. A child born mute would not be able to learn speaking so early. We don't remember but the first sound we must have heard as soon as we are born must be our own; may it be a loud cry or a movement of tongue.

Hornstein begins a Biographical article about Noam Chomsky with the following lines: "*Fish swim, birds fly, people talk..*" Communicating (mostly via speech) is a human need. A very few people can live a life without communicating. Hermits living their latter part of life in Himalayas too communicate. When two colleagues do not interact with each other after a big argument, the phrase used to describe their professional relationship status is "not on speaking terms". We do not say 'they aren't on listening terms' or 'they aren't on communication terms'. Speaking is a proof of our willingness to initiate or continue interaction.

Speaking is communicating, not necessarily other way around. One of the biggest achievements of evolved humans is development of languages and ability to speak. For millions of years, humans have been managing to avoid their extinction mainly because of extraordinary capability of communicating using sign language (as in covert military operations), spoken language, and machine language. So much so that humans have made arrangements to leave messages for aliens in case of probable extinction. This leads to the question – what the use of speaking is if the listeners (e.g., aliens) are not going to understand the communications. We don't only speak with ourselves, mostly we speak with others. So, we need to make sure that our spoken words are comprehended, especially at workplace. Communications at workplace is very formal and systematic.

Speaking is not just throwing words and sentences out and feel that *I have done my job, now whatever you want to understand is your job*. Action of speaking has reaction(s). Speaking is a skill which includes speaking with the reaction in mind. Most of the time, in formal communication set up, we remember how others should speak to us but forget how we should speak to others. Not only listening but also speaking demands empathy. When we listen to others, we give respect; when we speak, we get respect. We cannot speak with our colleagues like politicians do during their campaigning. The politicians can throw beautiful sentences and narratives in nice tones and shun the media asking tough questions but people working in corporate need to speak with responsibility and courage.

Initiation or Response

Like telephonic conversations, reasons for our speaking can also be incoming and outgoing; meaning we speak to either initiate the communication or respond to a communication. Let us call it initiated speaking and responded speaking. The former is about speaking because we want to get response while later is about speaking because we want to give response. In most of occasions, initiated speaking takes time while responsive speaking is quick. Sometimes we are so quick to respond that we don't even think before speaking. Most of the people in corporate hesitate to speak most of the time they are in front of their superiors or public.

Whether we need to speak to initiate a communication or respond to one, speaking needs preparation (as advised *watch your words*) at least for a couple of seconds because what is listened to can be ignored but not what is spoken. Not apologizing for speaking something wrong is worse than not thinking before opening mouth. Speaking demands office manners too. Corporate sees it is as a good etiquette when one seeks others' permission before speaking to them. This etiquette is applicable to talking to all the levels of hierarchy. Speak only when listener is ready. We must not just walk in to anyone and start conversation even though our colleagues are in the middle of something. One must not treat all the colleagues having similar preferences and habits of communication. For example, some (talkative) colleagues would like to listen to you while others would prefer that you just drop a text message or voice message. We must not assume that every colleague is always ready to listen to others/us. When one walks in to one's colleague and the colleague is on phone, one must definitely wait but one should also not start speaking to the colleague as soon as the colleagues puts down the phone. People need time to shift from one conversation to the other. People need to recollect first conversation, take mental or physical notes, and be prepared for the next conversation. Do not make people say, 'one moment please'. Another etiquette while speaking is avoiding overreacting. We need to mind not only our words but also our volume and facial expression. Speaking is art to decide how loudly or softly to speak, when and how much to smile while speaking, when to pause and when to stop speaking.

Etiquette and Manners

How do we speak is perhaps more important than what do we speak. Our tone and way of speaking touches people first and the words later.

Some believe (or have misbelief) that speaking fast gives the impression that speaker is fluent. Fluency in any language is not speaking speed only. Fluency has to do with using vocabulary, grammar, sentence structure, and thinking while speaking. Fluency is not measured by spoken wpm (words per minute). Fluency is just impressive but not useful if it does not help listeners to understand, think and response. Though corporate world is perceived for and known for impressing, usefulness of communication gets counted at the end.

Another misconception is about accent. In multinational corporations, employees try to imitate foreign accent with a belief that it will make the communication better and they will win the conversation. One needs to assure that listeners of one's accent must not feel being mocked. Therefore, speaking involves consideration of reactions and responses from listeners.

A very important aspect of initiating oral communication is addressing colleagues. Now, this depends on culture. For example, in the western culture, addressing superiors with their first name is a common practice while addressing them as 'sir' is not very common while in the eastern world 'sir' is widely practiced and addressing superiors with their first name is an insult.

Corporate settings witness blame-games and scapegoating very often. While speaking, one must be careful using the words 'you' and 'your'. The moment we say, '*you* deal with it.', 'it was *your* plan.', 'it is *your* fault.'; it becomes personal attack rather remarks to a person. Listeners take it seriously and personally. The alternative to avoid 'you' and 'your' is to use such words as 'we' and 'our'. But sometimes one would not like to hear 'we' and 'our', especially when one has achieved something all alone and would not like to see the credit of one's work being shared as 'we' or 'our'. In this case, use of passive voice comes to help. Moreover, one should be careful using the word 'we' also. 'We' is different from 'we all'. For example, when top management says, '*We are your friends.*', one must ask who are '*we*'? and why there is a need to use '*we*'? Sometimes 'we' is purposefully used in place of 'we all'. For example, saying 'We will find our amicable solution of this issue...' means not we all (you excluded) but only we few people will give the solution.

Speaking Types

Table 4: Speaking Types

Speaking types	*Preparation required*	*Mindfulness required*	*Reactions/ Response*	*Examples/situations*
Silence	None	None	Not important	Not participating in the discussion at departmental meetings.
Passive speaking	High	Low	Less important	Reading out policy/procedure to a colleague.
Involved speaking	Low	High	Very important	Describing your memorable experience at work.

Source: Authors' presentation.

Imagine three situations – (1) not speaking or participating in a conversation, (2) reciting rules and regulation or set of procedure to a colleague, who cannot read legal language, (3) describing your memories at a farewell gathering at office. These three situations can be described as (1) silence, (2) passive speaking, and (3) involved speaking.

Speaking types are based on occasions. Sometimes people avoid speaking in certain occasions such as meetings because they have experienced that whenever they have spoken or participated in discussion, it had gone against them. Speaking from a document can be seen as passive speaking. Here the speaker reads out the content of document (e.g., speech, rules, agenda, etc.). This is not actually talking. The speaker mostly reads and hardly thinks. The touchy and impactful communications are the one where the speakers speak naturally and with mindfulness.

Silence can have multiple reasons. Two main reasons are lack of willingness and lack of ability to speak. Speaking must be willing. Silence or non-participation from employees is most of the time adverse for organisations. Ability can be developed in some time but willingness takes long to develop and still it is hard to say whether willingness is developed. Lack of ability is related to physical challenges or lack of skill. To develop willingness to speak among the silent or nonparticipating people is tough because first – it is very difficult to make them aware that they are not participating. Not participating might have become normal for them. Second – it is difficult to know why people avoid participating in conversations. Thirdly – no skill development training programme or speech therapy would help to impart willingness to speak because the willingness is result of expectations and experiences. For example, if you are not expected (or not allowed) to speak, you will not be willing to speak despite having ability to speak. Generally, people avoid speaking unexpectedly or extempore. For self-respect, we avoid participating in discussion, in which we are not expected to. We avoid sharing ideas or suggestions and prefer to remain silent when we foresee being insulted and ignored.

Passive speaking is not telling. It is just presenting written words in verbal communication format. Unfortunately, in schools, families, or workplace, we have not properly taught the difference between speaking and orating. We speak less to receive responses and more to impress. We present ordinary ideas and use mediocre words in showy ways. We work so hard on how to speak that we forget the essence or matter of what we say. Communicating for business (for selling or marketing) works on impressions and presentations. It is mostly verbal presentation of content prepared well in advance. Most of the narrating way of communications lacks creativity. One can read out prepared speeches or speak out prepared Power Point slides but it would sound rehearsed not conversed.

Natural and unrehearsed words spoken from heart touches listeners and do not sound artificial or mechanically spoken. Active speaking is one in which the speakers speak with mindfulness and involvement. Most of the content delivered in active speaking is spontaneous. The intention in active speaking is to care for reaction or response of listeners, not just finish speaking agenda. The speakers need to pause during the communication to check whether the listener is affected by the speech or not and changes the speaking strategy.

What type of speaker am I? Is not as appropriate a question as *what type of speaking do I practice?* Speaking should be identified in types, not speakers. As described in the *Listening* section, Johari window model can become useful understanding one's speaking type.

One's goal should be to transit from passive speaking to active speaking. This transition does not happen overnight. One must develop certain skills to make this transition happen. Speaking skills get developed with paying attention to listening first. We learn to speak by keeping our eyes and ears open. A good speaker must be a good listener first. Careful observation on how others speak helps a lot. Active speaking becomes possible through pondering upon what to speak. After one is prepared with what to speak, one can go to the next step of how to speak, and then where and when to speak. As we get tired of listening to someone too long, others too get tired of our speaking too long. When to speak is important to know but more important to know is when to stop speaking. Silence is better than unwelcomed speech.

Many organisations like the people who speak less, ask no question, and mind their business with their head down. Organisations often forget that employee's silence is more harmful for organisations than their giving opinions, asking questions, and raising voice. Leaders should first worry about silence among employees. It is very common for corporate to train its employees on how to speak. Training on when and why to break the silence is rare in corporate. It is the organisation and its leaders who must make the transition from silence to active speaking among people possible. Creating silence culture is like a volcano ready to burst one day. That day the burst does larger devastation.

One of the misconceptions in corporate world regarding speaking is speaking with much respect (sometimes too much respect) to superiors and with low respect and with authority with subordinates. We have forgotten the concept of 'due respect'. This discrimination in speaking with different levels of seniors asks for lot of unnecessary energy and efforts to adjust levels of kindness in words. The easier (and kinder) way is to use equal and good respectful words for everyone without judging their hierarchy.

Speaking is more about thinking and feeling rather than about language and expression. Hence, the barriers in speaking would be more of mental barrier rather language barrier. Mental barriers are related with thinking/feeling and behaviour of the speakers and listeners. Very common barrier in speaking is to convince oneself to speak. It is not easy to find the answer of the question – *why should I speak to that person?* This question must be answered before we decide the content and message of what we are going to speak. Also, spoken communication cannot be effective when speaker needs to say a lot but listeners want to listen nothing. Choice of not speaking is sometimes situational too. For example, you want to talk to your colleague and you know what to say but looking at your colleagues disturbed mood or shouting on phone, you decided that it is not the right time to talk. The interpersonal relations too play role in making speaking a successful communication. Language barrier can be overcome quickly with the help of an interpreter but mental barrier cannot be overcome so quickly.

Speaking Between the Lines

Speaking between the lines is conveying underlying meanings using indirect and disguised words. Speaking between the lines is not much used phrase. There are only two entry on Google Scholar with "Speaking between the lines" in the title of the entry. One is the book by Susan Mandala, titled *Twentieth-century drama dialogue as ordinary talk: speaking between the lines*. The second entry is found in the review on this book.

In the situation where there is a risk of having adverse effect of using direct and blunt words in front of listeners, the messages are spoken out between the lines. For example, an employee asks the superior permission to work longer than usual hours. The superior is not ready to provide extra resources such as security guard or electricity. The superior would not show that he does not want to spend extra on resources and at the same time does not want to reveal this to the employee. So, he would tell all the reasons and risk of working extra such as not getting paid for overtime. The superior has spoken between the lines. Without denying the employee's request officially, he has achieved his goal or agenda. Most of the time 'between the lines' works but there are risks too.

There are two risks of speaking between the lines – one is listeners not getting the hidden message and the other is listeners misunderstanding the hidden message. In the former case, speakers can decode the hidden message to make listeners understand 'between the lines' part but in later case, it is not easy to treat the misunderstanding already happened. The listeners may react unexpectedly as a consequence of the misunderstanding happened. Communications should be direct. Instead of creating situation, where one has to speak between the lines, organisation must work on framing and implementing policies where communications remain direct and open.

Many miscommunications, employee dissatisfaction, and grievances occur due to lack of policies or unfair policies or biased policies, especially communication policies. One's 'voice' must not be filtered through the hierarchy before it reaches to the organisations' leaders.

The objective of speaking is not to silent others and dominate conversation. Speaking must make others speak. Unfortunately, the newly joined employees, have passed through group discussion process as part of admission to management graduate programmes, where they have been trained to dominate the discussion and impress the judge. During their management studies too, the future manager and leaders are not groomed for speaking but they are expected to be good at speaking. So, instead of training, judging begins. After completing degree programmes, the freshers join the corporate and still they carry with them the mindset of impressing and dominating the conversation. Corporate expect employees to be good at negotiating with candidates in job interviews, with employees, with clients, and with partners. Hence, the whole objective of speaking turns selfish and loses win-win approach.

Levels of Openness in Communications

Openness is a proof of transparency, trust, and positive work environment. But for some organisations and their leaders, Openness in communications is a threat as open communications do not allow them to complete their hidden agendas. How and up to what extent open communications are practiced depends on intentions and candidness of the leaders of organisations. Organisations' many agenda can be completed with covert communications but there are risky repercussions when covert communications remain no more covert. Because of grapevine communication is almost impossible to prevent at workplace, covert communications hardly remain covert.

Open Communications

When there is no secret and everyone in the organisation has equal access to the communications, the communications can be called the open communication. The communications can be made open by the way of formal announcements made to all. Open communication is inclusive and healthy communication.

Confidential Communications

Some communications in organisations are not made for everyone but at the same time not limited to one or two people only. When communication is accessible to a certain group of people, it can be called confidential communication. This confidentiality in communications is maintained to maintain business secrets, to protect intellectual property, or to save a large group of people facing panic situations.

Concealed Communications

Concealed communication is dangerous one. Here the information is shared among a few by a few. There is no larger benefit of concealed communications. Mostly, this is practiced to benefit a few in organisations. Sometimes, it is also practiced to gain personal benefits by hiding information from large group. Frequent use of phrases such as "It is between you and me only.", "Keep it to yourself.", etc. are signals that communications are concealed.

Receptive, Responsive, Reflective and Ruling Colleagues

With regards to communications, generally, we all experience four types of people at workplace – receptive, responsive, reflective, and ruling. Whether one likes or not, one has to deal with, work with, and live with these types of colleagues. We cannot change people to adjust to ourselves. Had people been able to change others, everyone would strive to change others ignoring changing oneself.

We could be any one of these four type of colleagues. Though there may not be solid exclusive categorisation. One may shift one's behaviour among being receptive, responsive, reflective, and ruling; depending on situation of, timing of, and person with who one is communicating.

Receptive people transmit (speak) less and are more interested in others' conversation. These colleagues like listen and learn rather than speak and teach. Receptive people are quick learners and do not like to interrupt when someone is speaking. Generally, they reflect once conversation is over, not during conversation. Receptive people have good memory.

Responsive people care to assure the speakers that they are listening. They keep analyzing speech and message while others are speaking but hardly interrupt. They speak or interrupt the conversation only to support or respond in yes/no. They like to keep the conversation short and like not to use many sentences if a few words can do.

Reflective people keep playing the conversation in their mind (sometimes for days) once the conversations are over. They are very sensitive people. One has to be careful using certain words in front of them. They can easily misunderstand the tone and messages spoken. Sometimes, they appear to be overthinking. They are good at analyzing speeches. They speak flawlessly and with intense preparations. Reflective people get irritated if interrupted while they are speaking.

Ruling people are dominating by nature. They hardly allow others to speak. They are conversation starters. They do not mind interrupting and often do not allow others to complete sentences. They speak like they are in elocution competition. Their speeches have less substance and more style. Ruling people possess very good convincing power but may irritate others if not trained when to pause or end the conversations.

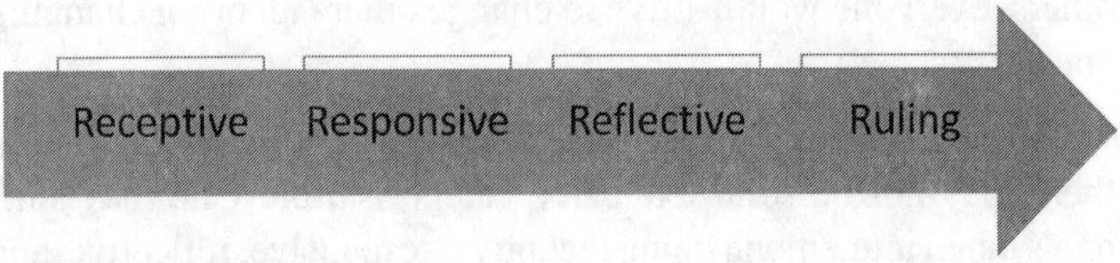

Source: Authors' presentation.

Figure 17: Types of Colleagues.

You need to ask yourself three questions:

1. What types of speakers are best?
2. What type of speaker you are?
3. What type of speaker you want to be?

When self-analysis or introspection does not help much, you must turn to your mentor (if available) or a trusted colleague, who can help you find answer of the above three questions. Do expect the mentor or the colleague to have the answers ready. They can help you find the answers to these questions rather finding them for you. We must not look for the shortcut to eat fish when someone is helping us learn how to catch a fish. Developing skill must be one's goal, not getting things done. Speaking is a skill that one should develop. No mentor or colleague can speak on behalf of you every time.

Honesty and Confidence

Speaking is different from speaking with confidence. An irony is in corporate (especially in marketing) it is taught that even if you tell a lie, tell with confidence to make it believable. This is either exaggerated or misinterpreted. The emphasis should have been on confidence but people see excuse to tell a lie with a weapon of confidence.

One cannot make everyone fool every time. A lie cannot sell nicely wrapped and packed in confidence. Cheap wine in a vintage bottle might sell but not satisfy buyers. Using tricks in speaking makes people ignore liars' fake confidence and look for truth in the words. Repetitions of lying (even with confidence) results in trust loss.

Another dangerous form of lying during conversations is hiding the truth or facts. Not telling what one should know too is dishonesty, which will not sustain business relations longer.

Using Right Words

Let us study a situation. Once a candidate introduced herself during job interview, the interviewer asked, "What does your father do?"

The candidate: "My father was a teacher."

The interviewer is wondering 'was' means her father is no more? How to confirm that?

This can be presented as – "My father is a retired teacher."

Another common phrase is "Where do you live?"

A better way of asking is "Where do you stay at?"

Speaking Exercises

1. Make a list of how many people did you speak today with?
2. To whom all you did speak today? What was the purpose of conversation?
3. Write about your first public speaking experience.
4. What do you regret speaking about? Why?
5. Among your colleagues, who do you appreciate as your speech model?
6. Write about an occasion or two, where you were forced to speak?
7. Request your colleague to give you any topic, give an extempore speech on the topic.
8. Ask your colleague to analyze your speaking type (silence, passive or active).
9. Ask your colleague whether you are receptive, responsive, reflective, or ruling speaker. Contemplate over the feedback received.

Reading

Reading has become so inevitable that we humans have invented Braille system, audio books, text-to-speech programmes, scan-and-translate, etc. to cure the reading inability or disability. Earlier literate people with reading ability were valued so much that some of them made a living reading for illiterates (see movie *News of the World*).

People working in corporate get exposed to reading a variety of messages containing range of length. Widely read communications are in forms of instructions, notes, memos, orders, circulars, advices, complaints, reports, policies, contracts – the list is exhaustive.

Reading is a receptive activity, like listening but it has one major advantage over listening i.e., revising or going back to what is read. One has to request with phrases like 'come again' or 'beg your pardon' if one misses out the said part while listening. If the person to whom one is listening is a strict teacher who warns 'listen carefully; I won't repeat' then the listener cannot go back to the said part. Reading has all the control given to the reader. This difference is due to medium of communications. We listen to people while read text (also multimedia). It is easier to adjust pace of reading text/documents compared to adjust speed and volume of the person speaking. It is easier to postpone completely stop reading a document, if reader wishes but in case of listening, the listener has to request or order to speaker to postpone or stop speaking. Reading medium obeys readers. Reading does not require the receivers of communications to show the senders of communications that the receivers are attentively receiving messages. One can sit back, relax, and read messages without being in front of the senders of messages.

Another advantage of reading is keeping record or underlining the text, which is very difficult in case of listening. However, reading has a disadvantage too i.e., reading needs verbal explanations, if the communication is not lucid. It is because the text lacks voice, tones, and expression; the reading sometimes becomes a boring communication. This is the reason why for some document, we read out loud to ourselves. Adding our speech while reading helps our brain to understand the tone of written words.

First impression in reading is length and importance. For example, when we see an email in our inbox, sent by colleague A, before opening the email, we can say that the message will be very long (mainly based on our experience); when we see an email sent by colleague B, we can say that the message will be very important. Just like you see a talkative colleague approaching you and you be prepared for very long conversation.

Reading is not an ability to read (literacy), it is a skill. Just like other skills, reading skills too can be sharpened. The skill gets improved with more and more reading. As a part of business communications, we do not read like we read newspaper but we read with an objective. We read to comprehend, to respond or ignore, to act upon, to follow the instruction, and to give instruction. In case readers do not understand part of written message and writers are not available to explain, the readers depend on their ability to comprehend the written communication, including guessing. Many times, we guess the meanings, especially when the writers use difficult words and figures of speech to make the communication impressive.

Reading and Word Power

Though vocabulary is generally considered as an important part of fluency, it plays a big role while reading too. For example, while reading a particular document, if one has to find meaning of many unfamiliar words frequently; it will not only eat up lot of time but also break the continuity and momentum while reading. Just one unfamiliar word sometimes makes us again and again read entire paragraph or sentence.

Though the internet and particularly search engines are just click away, the problem with search engines is they do not understand the context of the term/word searched very often. For example, if you read the sentence in a report "*The crowd boiled in frustration.*" you might get confused a little, if you have read use of the verb *boil* first time, like in this sentence. Try searching the word *to boil* on search engine online, you will not get such meaning of this word so quickly that you can comprehend this sentence. Probably, instead of spending time on finding meaning of the word *boil*, you would prefer to guess the meaning of that word by relating another word *frustration* in the same sentence and conclude that *boil* is used in a negative connotation here.

Mostly reading and interpreting legal terms and jargons tests one's reading skills. Instead of jumping to grab the dictionary or search the word on internet, one must try to confirm whether one has looked for the meaning of the word before or it is the first encounter with the alien word. If one has tried to search the unfamiliar word even once before, one must make an attempt to recall the meaning and if the memory fails, then online or printed dictionary should be used. Reading skills, especially vocabulary cannot be enhanced if we allow to grow the lazy and shortcut habit of searching for meaning or definition of unfamiliar words every time. One has to boil it hard. Dictionaries must not make us dependent or handicapped.

Typesetters (in consultation with publishers and authors) do not leave broad page margins in paperback books for no reason. The purpose is to allow the readers to take notes in addition to underline or highlight part of the text. Reading must be carried out with a pen or pencil handy. We think while we read and if we do not put our thoughts immediately on paper, they evaporate in fraction of a second. Secondly, we cannot rely on our memory to store and retrieve every minute communication we have read and so, there is a need to take notes. In addition to the purpose of recording and retrieving communicated messages, one more objective for note taking is to put on paper the readers' thought, comments, summary and understanding of the communications.

Types of Reading

Broadly, reading can be seen as causal and formal. These types mainly depend on purpose and matter of reading.

Casual Reading

Casual reading is reading for not so serious purpose. The purpose of reading casually is to relax, to kill time, to get yourself updated, to satisfy curiosity, to socialise, and to get entertainment. Casual reading is self-paced reading. Readers read according to their mood. No immediate action or reaction is required as a result of casual reading. Except for hobbies, it is not a common practice to keep records of what is casually read. Readers do not worry about authenticity of the writers. Examples of casual reading are news items, social media posts, advertisements, fiction work, etc.

Formal Reading

Formal reading is reading with serious objective. Formal reading happens mostly for work or study purpose. It is not leisurely reading. Formal reading is done keeping deadline in mind. Formal reading needs to be prioritised. Some action such as responding, acknowledging, and action (acting upon) is needed as a result of formal reading. Formal reading is not just for reading and forgetting; record keeping of written documents read is also a good practice. Reading legal contracts, study material (for job, promotion, driving licence, professional certification, etc.), official memos, reports, newsletters, etc. are examples of formal reading content.

Reading can also be categorised in the following four categories:

Glancing

Glancing is quickly reading first one or two sentences of paragraphs of documents. Glancing is practiced when the written communication is relatively lengthier or time to read entire document line by line is short.

Quick Reading

Readers do not skip anything in quick reading process, unlike in glancing. Quick reading is reading everything but without stopping by to think. Here, readers postpone the comprehension until entire message/document is not read once and in one go. Reading with a plan to read the message twice, if necessary, involves quick reading.

Slow Reading

Slow reading follows 'Do it right first time' principle. Slow reading is for absorbing everything read. All the words of the message are read carefully, nothing is skipped, and attempts are made to comprehend everything in the first attempt. This type of reading is used when the message (irrespective of its length) is complicated or containing technical language or when the readers are mandated to respond to the communication.

Revised Reading

Revising is reinforcing the read content. Here, readers read the message/document multiple times. All the above reading types may be parts of reinforcement. Revised reading becomes necessary when readers are supposed to memorise the content and present it later, e.g., plan, reports, results of activities, etc.

These categories are not alternative to one another. Any of these reading categories can be practiced depending on available time to read and prioritising of the messages based on importance given to the messages.

Context

It is of no use to read without knowing context but keep guessing what the content is about. Certain words have different contextual meanings. For example, while reading a crime report, you come across the phrase 'a charge of battery' and even if you search this phrase on internet, you might not get the right context[1]

Readers need to focus on the background of the content. Jargons are commonly used in communications in business and law. Newly recruited employees in public organisations are given book of administrative terms. This is not practiced much in corporate. Corporate expects that during studies, the MBAs, Chartered Accountants, and engineers must have learnt the management terms and jargons. Many miscommunications arise due to unfamiliarity with workplace jargons. Here are some of the widely used corporate jargons:

1. **Passing the buck:** Blaming or passing onus to others for one's mistake or failure.

   Generally, in corporate, people do not have courage to accept the results of their actions when the actions have negative outcomes. So, they pass the buck to others. Often the buck is passed to intern, newly recruited, or not so strong colleague.

2. **Back door entry:** Someone who is recruited violating ethics, rules, regulations, or procedure for recruitment.

   Corporate recruitments are not always fair and transparent. Much information is not available to public, unlike in case of public organisations. This jargon is used for an employee (i.e., she is a back door entry) and for corrupt system too (i.e., she is here through back door entry system).

3. **Bottleneck:** An action or individual(s), which delays the subsequent processes.

   When the process or decisions are linked and one slow link in the chain does not do its job on time, entire process delays. For example, a slow worker in an assembly line. There is a popular phrase used for top management people i.e., *bottleneck is always at the top of the bottle.*

4. **Brainstorming:** A group of people think together on one or more issue(s) to find a solution or explore opportunities.

   There are many ways such as asking, observing, experimenting, etc. to gather information and insight before taking decisions. Brainstorming in one of such ways, where a problem or issue is given to the group and the group members (generally, marketing team) think collectively to ding the solution.

5. **I am sitting on it:** It means 'I am working on it.'

   The task is not completed yet and I have not left working on it. It is the answer when someone asks status report of the given task. For example, the superior asks, "Did you prepare the report?". The subordinate replies, "No sir, I am sitting on it."

6. **Downsize:** Reducing the number of employees.

   Downsizing simply means firing or laying off a number of employees in a particular time span. Downsizing can be due to financial reasons or other reasons such as the employer is forced to shut down the business.

7. **Pink slip:** A notice given to employees about their termination or separation from employer.

   In earlier days, when notices were given to employees about termination of their job, these notices were given on a pink letter. Still some corporate print the notice on pink pages.

8. **Golden handshake:** A large sum of money (and other benefits) offered to employees whom employer gives pink slip before their retirement or resignation.

   As a part of contract or to compensate employees' earning lost due to their termination, employer offers such employee a good amount of money. Sometimes, with money other benefits such as a club membership, a car, or property is also offered.

9. **Working in silo:** Working in silos means working in isolation.

   Silos are large containers used to store material in farms or factories. This jargon is used when employees or departments do not interact with one another much and work in a water tight compartments. It is contrary to teamwork.

10. **Piggyback:** Someone (a child or sack) being transported on people's back is known as piggyback.

Metaphorically, the jargon piggybacking is used when someone takes credit of others' success or ideas. For example, if Ms. A prepares entire project report but Mr. B presents it to the superiors without giving credit to Ms. A, it is said that he has piggybacked on her efforts.

11. **Intimation:** It means announcement (from Latin *intimationem*) but the announcement is most of time indicative or hidden.

    When there is an indirect hint of someone's action, this jargon is used. For example, employee A's frequent absence can be an intimation about alcoholism. It is also used for notifying something too.

12. **Apprise:** To inform or update others about the progress of an event or task.

    This is not very commonly used term in corporate, it is used as alternate to *intimation*. The word has derived from Latin *apprehendere*, which means to inform or notify. For example, "We will carry out field investigation and apprise you about the incident."

13. **Scapegoat:** When someone innocent is framed and punished for others' fault, it is called scapegoating.

    The word has connection with the bible, in which, out of two goats, one was sacrificed and other 'scapegoat' lived. Often at workplace, innocent people are punished for others' mistakes due to lack of alertness or lack of evidence.

14. **Cash cow:** The product, department, or company with high revenue are known as cash cows.

    All the products, departments, or subsidiary companies do not give the same profit to the business group. Those products, departments, or companies earn higher revenue or profit are called cash cows. This revenue can be used for investing in other businesses or expanding existing ones.

15. **Superannuated:** The term literary means outdated and is used for stock/inventory.

    Surprisingly, along with stock or inventory, this jargon is used also for people! For example, Mr. A superannuated last year. When used for people, it means retired.

16. **Account:** This financial term is also used for clients or customers (in advertising business).

    Generally, the term account is used for maintaining financial records of a particular party, with which the organisation is dealing with but particularly, advertising agencies use this term for different companies, for which they make advertisements.

17. **You are Bangalored:** This means your job is given to someone accepting cheaper wages, generally in other countries.

    This jargon was born after a large number of American companies began outsourcing information technology work to other countries like in India. Bangalore became one of the most preferred spots for outsourcing jobs. Whenever someone in the U.S. will lose the job to outsourcing, it would be said, 'You are Bangalored.'

18. **Induction:** Making newly recruited employees familiar with organisation and its people, culture, policies, rules, resources, etc.

    The jargon induction can be confused with the induction process in electric devices. In corporate, induction means making newly joined people acquainted with the organisation. In some corporate, induction lasts for a week or fifteen days. Induction is provided in form of training too.

19. **Advice (to banks):** When an instruction or request is sent to the bank, generally about bulk payments by employers, it is called advice to bank.

In banking system, an advice is sent to the banks by the employers with a list of their employees, their account numbers, and the amount of salary to be deposited in the employees bank account.

20. **Just In Time:** Just In Time is a philosophy advocating arrival or resource neither early nor late at the required place.

    Of course, late arrival of resources such as raw material, human resources, financial resource, etc. delays production and distribution of goods but early arrival is a waste of time too. JIT is a Japanese philosophy, which advocates arrival of resources at the place required, neither early nor late.

21. **Hire-and-fire:** It refers to short-term employment.

    In many countries, business laws mandates employers to provide employees with long term service benefits such as pension or gratuity. To save on offering benefits to employees for their long service, some employers recruit and separate them in a few years.

22. **Wear and tear:** It means that damage or wearing out of stuff due to routine, regular, or normal use of the stuff.

    This is widely used term in warranty terms. Manufactures excluded normal damage or wear out of the goods from the warranty provided because damage or wear out is not a manufacturing faulty and also it causes due to the users' actions.

23. **In letter and in spirit:** Meaning actually acting upon as instructed or agreed upon.

    When the instruction is to follow the order not just for completing formality but actually implementing the ordered action, this jargon is used. Intent is important here.

24. **Climbing the corporate ladder:** Getting promotions, advancing in career, going up in hierarchy in corporate.

There is a metaphorical ladder in corporate. Everyone gets motivated going up in the hierarchy. When someone gets promoted quickly or without delay, the term climbing up the ladder is used.

25. **Insubordination:** Not following superior's order or instruction or not obeying superior's command.

    Like in military organisation, many corporate put his insubordination clause as a service rule, that the employee has to follow. There are sever punishments such as separation from the organisation too for not obeying the superior's orders or instructions.

Getting ourselves familiarised with frequently used corporate jargons and taking the context in reference, we can better comprehend the office communications. This is the matter of practice. The more we read, the better communicator we become.

Reading Office Communications

While reading the formal communications, we tend to first look at who is the sender. Our context is half set when we know about the sender. Communications from superiors are in tone and form of instruction or order while communications from subordinates are in the tone and form of reporting or request. Very often we can say what the message would be like before even opening or completely reading the message. We virtually keep the sender in front of our eyes while reading the sent message.

The task and purpose of reading does not end with completing reading the message unless and until the message is interpreted in their meaning. Reading without interpretation is hearing but not listening. Interpretation depends on many aspects such as conveyed meaning, inferred meaning, knowledge, expectations between senders and receivers of communications, experiences of senders and receivers, etc.

Even written messages can have miscommunications, if there is a gap between conveyed meaning and inferred meaning. It is very difficult to pass the judgment on whose fault it is in case of miscommunication. The onus lies on sender as well as receiver to foresee probable miscommunication and avoid it.

Empathetic reading helps to make communications do its job effectively. Here, empathy means senders put themselves in receivers' shoes and vice a versa. Still, miscommunications are unavoidable. After every incident of miscommunication, we tend to think who went wrong instead of what went wrong. Putting aside blame-game, if the senders and receiver sit and discuss the nitty gritty of the miscommunication, the future occurrences of miscommunication can be reduced, if not brought down to zero.

Reading and Digital Devices

With the advent of technology, reading is shifting from paper to screen. Reading on devices has its own advantages and disadvantages. Despite enormous storage capacities of reading devices, we have not completely forgotten the traditional book-reading habit. The reading devices (e-book readers, tablets, smart phones, laptops, etc.) not only add to the eye strain but also lack the joy of underlining, highlighting, dog-earing, and writing notes (including our names) on printed materials. Though modern reading devices have a few features such as bookmarking, highlighting, and searching particular words, these devices have not been able to completely replace papers. One of the biggest advantages of using reading devices is the ability of devices to share the documents with less time and cost.

On devices, we read offline and online content with different length and characteristics. The length ranges from extensive text document to short comments on online social media platforms. Generally, on online social media, extensive content is discouraged mainly due to audience losing interest in reading long posts. For example, earlier, when users typed or pasted long (more than 420 character) content in the Facebook Status, it asked the users to convert it into a note. Also, Twitter allowed 140 character for many years. Almost similar character limit has been imposed for using SMS services.

Time, cost, and convenience to access multi-media content (image, videos, animation, etc.) are the greatest advantage to use electronic devices for reading purpose. Of course, images can be printed on paper and be communicated as a part of written document but it will add in time and cost of printing as well as it will not be as presentable as digital format.

Table 5: Reading Printed and Digital Content

	Reading printed content	***Reading digital content***
Time to access	High	Low
Cost to access	High	Moderate
Convenience to access	Low	High

Source: Authors' presentation.

Digital mode of communication is faster, cost effective, and convenient not only for reading the messages but also responding those. Due to convenience to reply quickly using devices, one might be tempted to reply instantly but one must not unless it is the case of urgency. Instant replies take away responders' time to think before responding. Unfortunately, digital communications have created an impression that the communication is urgent. All high-speed communications may not be urgent or important ones. Receivers of the digital messages must understand that there are features such as *read receipts* or *delivery notifications*, which effortlessly inform the senders of communications about messages being delivered. So, there is no need to hastily or instantly replying order to prove that one has received, read, and working on the communications.

Reading Between the Lines

Let's see a hypothetical situation. Mr. A has been given a task to convert numbers and figures into charts and present it in the meeting tomorrow. A sends the message to Mr. B - 'Will you help me with charts?' Notice that A has not written 'Will you show me how to make charts?' B must 'read between the lines' that A wants B to make charts for him; A does not want or does not have time to learn from B how to make charts. The 'between the lines' message here is A wants to get the work done through B, for which B might not get any credit. There are many such written messages, which explicitly do not communicate, rather readers are supposed to read the underlying meanings and interpret them. There are several such communications, where the readers are expected to read between the lines. The purpose of implicit messages is to save the readers from any trouble from putting anything on record. In the above example, A does not want that it goes on record that he did not prepare charts himself but B did the job on A's behalf.

Saying 'no' is widely read between the lines. Generally, 'no' of rejection does not directly begin with "we are sorry to write to you that..." or "we regret to inform you that...". In the following communication, see how the bank is indirectly denying the requested refund and asking the customer for more document:

Dear Dr. Vyas,

Thank you for your email. We understand your request for refund from ABC merchant.

We would like to inform you that when transactions fail, the transaction amount gets credited to the customers' bank account.

However, as per previous communication email kindly provide us with the Complaint Form to present it to the merchant to initiate the refund process.

In case you have any other queries, you can call us on our toll-free number 1800-xxx-xxxx.

Best Regards,

G Ramaswamy
Customer Support
XYZ Bank

Here follows one more communication asking for more information at the end of the email rather beginning with 'sorry, we can't help you without required information':

> Dear Chaitanya,
>
> We are sorry to know that you are unable to access our internet services.
>
> This is not kind of experience we would like our valued service users to undergo and we are sorry to see our customers facing inconvenience.
>
> Rest assured that we are working to solve your problem as soon as possible.
>
> Please share your complete address with house number, building name, street, area, city, and zip code number where you faced service unavailability. These details will help us understand the issue and serve you better.
>
> Thank you.

The above communications are the examples of how to read between the lines.

Reading to Grow and Excel

The biggest challenge for those working in corporate is not the fact that the business world is changing the challenge is it is changing so fast that every day one has to run fast to keep pace with the time. Sometimes, twenty-four hours in a day are not enough to pause, think, and plan for getting success in corporate world. Reading is not only skill but also power. The power to (survive,) grow, and excel in one's career at corporate. We are living in the information age. Information and knowledge, along with skills and attitude, are the drivers to progress and prosperous.

We need to practice reading beyond the gamut of official communications such as notices, memos, instructions, contract, etc. We need to enter the zone of reading for *food for thought*. Avoiding reading affects ability to think in correct direction.

Reading is the habit which changes readers' other habits, thinking, and personality. Many successful people in corporate share about their reading habits and the books they read. We should read the books written by people who are working in corporate sectors, if not by philosophers or religious gurus. One can search the internet for the following to get the book list:

- books recommended by entrepreneurs
- books successful people read
- business philosophy books
- CEO reading list
- fortune 500 reading list

Here are some of the popular titles for reading:

- *Blue Ocean Strategy* by W. Chan Kim and Renée Mauborgne
- *Deep Work: Rules for Focused Success in a Distracted World* by Cal Newport
- *Getting Things Done: The Art of Stress-Free Productivity* by David Allen
- *Great by Choice: Uncertainty, Chaos, and Luck—Why Some Thrive Despite Them All* by Jim Collins
- *Rich Dad, Poor Dad* by Robert Kiyosaki
- *Shoe Dog* by Phil Knight
- *The 4 Disciplines of Execution: Achieving Your Wildly Important Goals* by Chris McChesney, Sean Covey and Jim Huling
- *The E-Myth* by Michael Gerber
- *The Hard Thing About Hard Things* by Ben Horowitz

There are avid readers in business world, who have developed themselves by finding a mentor in the books. Reading is a beacon (of light) in the dark side of corporate (with some exceptions) full of politics, power, race, rivalry, and revenge.

Reading Exercises

1. From a business newspaper, list down words or jargons you have never come across before.
2. Count the documents you have read on any device in last week.
3. Out of document you have read on devices in last week, could you contain multimedia (image, video, animation, etc.)?
4. Do you read all the emails one by one or you prioritise them?
5. Think about any message you have read but have misunderstood.
6. Which were some difficult words you read and searched their meaning in online or printed dictionary?
7. Search for the meaning of the word w*orkaholic*.
8. Which were some of the communications you read which did not say yes/no directly but made you read between the lines?
9. Which business book you like the most? What it is about?
10. What do you like in the business book you like the most?

Writing

Many believe that people are born with the gift of writing and to support this belief, people quote examples of famous writers or orators writing their speech on their own. One such personality often mentioned is Abraham Lincoln, for whom many believed that he was a gifted orator, who could write his great speeches within a snap of fingers.

Was Lincoln a Gifted and Genius Orator?

"A notion persists to this day that Lincoln was such a gifted oratorical genius that he could write speeches on a whim, including the Gettysburg Address. Scholarship over the past decade has

dispelled this fallacy, noting that Lincoln was uncomfortable in making impromptu or extemporaneous speeches."..."His drafts included numerous revisions and editing comments, usually found in strike-outs, underlining words he wanted to emphasize before an audience, and an abundance of handwritten comments written in the side margins."[2]

Writing is most formal and needs extra attention among all four skills (listening, speaking, reading, writing). Writing involves process of framing the messages, putting them down on paper or in digital format, and transmitting the messages. We can see that from Gayla's above findings.

Because written communications are records and the writers or the senders cannot refute on occurrence or content of the communications, the senders will have to be more careful before transmitting the written words. Fortunately, writing has an option to reframe the content before communicating. One can write, re-write, read again and again and can also correct it if necessary. This process helps make the communication more formal. This feature is not available in case of spoken communications. The speaker cannot speak, judge how the spoken words sound, and then correct the words, if necessary. 'Words cannot be taken back' is true for spoken words, not for written ones. People playing politics in office know that words are like sped arrows so they do not deny that communication happened but they deny on matter and content of the messages.

Most of the communications at workplace happen verbally. So much that in certain organisations, meetings are called without sending written intimations and agenda; even minutes are not considered to be sent as report. In the lack of written communications and in the name of informal meetings, white-collar workers sometimes feel like a supervisor who whistles his blue-collar construction workers to call for a quick round of instructions. Writing is not as convenient as speaking.

Here too, hierarchy plays a major role. It is obvious and well-accepted that superiors communicate verbally and subordinates write (take notes) the messages, not the other way around. Superiors can conveniently forget the subordinates' verbal requests but subordinates cannot forget superiors' verbal commands. This is the unwritten rule in some organisations.

Unlike speaking, writing, especially in corporate communications, does not begin with 'Hi' or 'I was wondering...' or 'I just wanted to talk about...' or 'We need to talk'. There is a way or etiquette to frame the written messages. Some of the common phrases to begin formal written messages (after salutation) are shown below:

"Thanks for your email."

"Thank you for your reply, I really appreciate that."

"With reference to the trailing email…"

"Hope this email finds you well."

"Thank you for your interest in our organisation"

"This is to inform you…"

"It has brought to our notice that…"

"An item you ordered has been dispatched."

Two things we need to kept in mind while writing in a correct way – one, words are not written as they are spoken; and two, synonyms cannot be used alternatively. We (incorrectly) use certain words to emphasize or under influence of other languages we know. For example, one must avoid using 'different different', 'etc. etc.', 'go go', and such words spoken in informal conversation. We should not write the way we speak. Secondly, we must be careful using synonym. We tend to use alliterations and rhyming words to make writing look more effective. This might change the meaning. Many are not sure when to write the word 'sorry'. 'Sorry' is not an apology word. It means the person is sad and expresses sympathy but not apologizing. For example, using the phrase 'sorry for your loss' in a condolence note. Here the word 'sorry' in the note shows sadness, not apology. When one should take responsibility of failure or adverse event, one must write 'I apologize', not just 'I am sorry'.

Let us read an incident on a lighter note:

A student to a professor: "Professor, when can we use 'I am sorry' but not 'I apologize'?

The witty professor, known for his brevity, replied, "At funerals".

Another widely used and misinterpreted word is 'so called'. In India, there was a big cry out against the New York Times, when the NYT used the word 'so called playback singer' to describe Indian singer Lata Mangeshkar. People believe that the word 'so called' is used in derogatory terms for the legendary singer of India. For example, "that so called writer has published only one book", "that so called yoga-guru doesn't know anything about yoga." We do not understand that 'so called' means 'called that way'. The newspaper may not know what a 'playback singer' is because western cinemas don't have songs in the middle of the story where hero and heroine lip sync dancing around trees on a hill! So, the newspaper wanted to introduce to the readers the concept of playback singing and that Mangeshkar is a playback singer. What if an Indian newspaper ('so called' mobile journalist) writes "Jinping, so called Premier of China ...' means the newspaper wants to introduce its readers that Prime Ministers in China are called Premier. It is no way objectionable.

It is observed that writing is avoided if verbal communications can do the job. There are to reason for avoiding – (1) because writing is tedious compared to speaking, and (2) because some communications are off the record.

It is easier to communicate verbally rather than putting it on paper. This is obvious reason to minimize written communication at workplace. Not so obvious reason to avoid written communication is to keep the communication off the record. Writers or senders of communications see probable threat of communication being made on the record because of many reasons such as hiding information, benefitting certain people, not revealing business secret or plan, etc. As far as communications related to business secret or intellectual property rights are concerned, keeping the communications off the record is explicable but if the agenda is to hide information or to share information with certain people (e.g., insider trading), then this action leads to the loss of transparency and fairness in organisational communications. On the contrary, when verbal communications may show chances of communications being slipped out of mind or denied having occurred, written communication becomes a must. Spoken words may be denied their existence but written words cannot be.

One more purpose of written communications is that it works as a manual, a rule book, or a set of guidelines. An employee not very familiar to the organisation processes and systems should not approach the superior or colleagues for every procedural query. For this purpose, a written communication works as a standing instruction or a lighthouse.

In Promulgating your Esoteric Cogitations

As far as possible business writing should be free from excessive use of figures of speech and wit. Decorative language is redundant in business communications. Some have flare for using perceived sophisticated and fancy word to make an impression. For example, using hardly used phrase 'I second your opinion'. After a meeting, Ms. A writes an email to all present in the meeting, proposing a transparency policy about allowing all the employees to access performance appraisals and confidential reports of others. On this, Mr. B writes back – 'I second that'. Mr. B could have written 'I agree' or 'I support that'. The phrase 'I second that' is used in a parliamentary procedure of motions. The second person to support a motion uses this phrase. But surprisingly, in office communications; third, fourth, and all who agree write 'I second that'!

Why should such phrases be avoided outside parliament? There are three reasons – one, not everyone understands such phrases; two, there are easier and more familiar phrases available, which are widely used in place of such phrases; and three, use of big words to look smart may have opposite effect.[3]

Read the following passage:

"In promulgating your esoteric cogitations, or articulating your superficial sentimentalities and amicable, philosophical, or psychological observations, beware of platitudinous ponderosity. Let your conversational communications possess a clarified conciseness, a compacted comprehensibleness, a coalescent consistency, and a concatenated cogency. Eschew all conglomerations of flatulent garrulity, jejune babblement, and asinine affectation. Let your extemporaneous descantings and unpremeditated expatiations have intelligibility and veracious vivacity, without rhodomontade, or thrasonical bombast. Sedulously avoid all polysyllabic profundity, pompous prolixity, psittaceous vacuity, ventriloquial verbosity, and vaniloquentvapidity. Shun double entendres, prurient jocosity, and pestiferous profanity, obscure or apparent."

The above 90-words long communication can be expressed in five words – 'do not use big words'.

Writing for Receivers

Before initiating written communication, the sender should keep in mind the receiver of the communications. One may be an extraordinary writer of technical reports or manuals but if the audience is freshmen or sophomores then the language must be very simple.

If written communications are to be sent in form of attachment, they must be accompanied with a cover letter. Documents sent without cover letters keep the receivers wondering who has sent the documents? Why? What the sender wants from me? Why should

I respond?, etc. There are two occasions, which demand writing skilful cover letters – (1) applying for a job position or promotion, and (2) writing to conduct research. Writing for these occasions are explained below:

Letter with job or promotion application

Writing cover letter is an art. Most of us either don't feel need to attaching cover letter or don't know how to write effective cover letter, especially when apply for a position or promotion in any organisation. Cover letter is not just a courteous gesture but also sets the context and purpose of communications made in the attachment of resume or such other documents presented for a position. Resume is just a list of qualifications, credentials, and achievements while cover letter 'talks' to the recruiter or committee. Common but essential elements in cover letter are:

1. Date
2. Receiver's name and address
3. Subject
4. Reference
5. Salutation
6. Opening paragraph
7. Body of the letter
8. Closing note
9. Gratitude
10. Sender's signature and name

Letter with questionnaire

Another very commonly expected cover letter in business communications is with the questionnaire used for surveys. Whether sent via mail or emails, questionnaire must be accompanied with a cover letter. The sample cover letter and its elements are shown below:

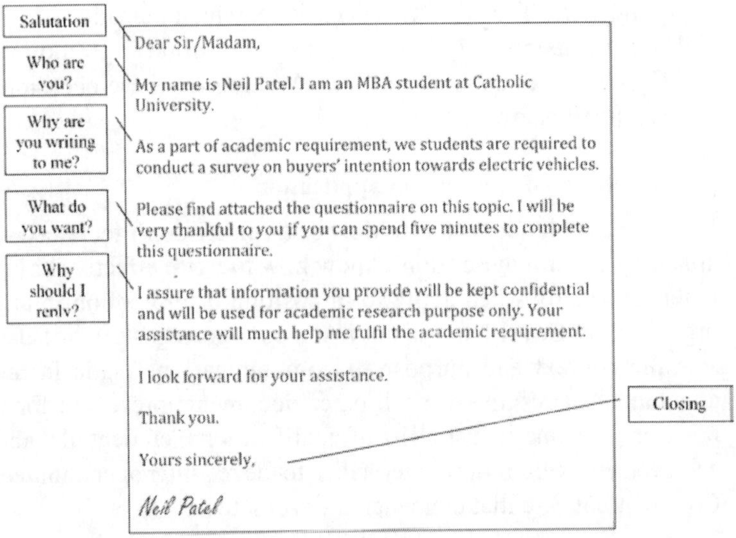
Dear Sir/Madam,

My name is Neil Patel. I am an MBA student at Catholic University.

As a part of academic requirement, we students are required to conduct a survey on buyers' intention towards electric vehicles.

Please find attached the questionnaire on this topic. I will be very thankful to you if you can spend five minutes to complete this questionnaire.

I assure that information you provide will be kept confidential and will be used for academic research purpose only. Your assistance will much help me fulfil the academic requirement.

I look forward for your assistance.

Thank you.

Yours sincerely,

Neil Patel

Different written business communications have different receivers or stakeholders. Stakeholders are any individual or group directly or indirectly related with business organisations. Some of the examples of communications to stakeholders are as explained below:

Communications	Stakeholders
Annual reports	Investors
Compliance reports	Regulatory authorities
Memorandum	Employees
Agreements	Associates
Licencing agreements	Dealers/distributors
Marketing communications	Customers or prospects

1. **Annual Reports:** Annual reports are written by companies mainly for shareholders or investors. Annual reports are information and impression given to the investors about company and its performance. The content is more about how company performed in previous year. The financial performance is emphasized along with how the company

is contributing to society. There should be two major objectives of writing annual reports – (1) To show the investors that their investments made are justified, and (2) assure the investors that their future investments will be worth making. Annual reports are not written creatively but there is certain mandatory information to be included, as prescribed by government/regulator.

2. **Compliance reports:** There are various compliances for businesses to report to regulatory agencies. Some of these compliances are financial, environmental, and legal at large. Business organisations need to fulfil these compliances and report them in detail. The communication form is again reporting, like in annual reports but here, the communication is for various government agencies, not shareholders. Two major aspects in compliance reports are evidence and details.

3. **Memorandum:** Memorandum (called memo) are intended for internal communications i.e., communication among organisation's employees only. To write about important decisions, suggestions, complaints, justifications/ explanation, etc. memorandum are used. Generally, memorandum is in short document format. Newsletters are more informative rather reporting. Newsletters may be put on organisations' website for public and are communicated with a fixed time interval (fortnightly, monthly, bimonthly, etc.). Newsletters are one of the few business communications, which has a lot of images about activities, charts, diagrams, etc.

4. **Agreements:** Business organisations require so many agreements to be drafted by almost every day that a separate team with skills of drafting legal documents is needed. These agreements can be between supplier and manufacturer, buyer and seller, partners, dealers/ distributors, and also purchase order. Writing or drafting agreements requires understanding of laws and ability to

envisage potential conflict. So, one has to be careful with using words. For example, very common word used to describe something not free is *paid* (this is free but that is paid). Actually, the word *payable* should be used. Else, paid means someone has made payment for it.

5. **Marketing Communications:** Because marketing is a profit centre, the communication done by this function should be designed with utmost care. Communication from other business functions (finance, H.R., production, operations, and I.T.) normally are internal while very large magnitude of marketing communications are transmitted to public. The myopic understanding about marketing communications is advertising. Because marketing is not just advertising or selling, marketing communications too are not limited to these two. Marketing communications encompasses not only advertising but also sales promotions, direct marketing, publicity, personal selling, Public Relations, and digital marketing. Marketing communication needs to be customised according to its transmitting media. Media carrying written marketing communications are print (newspaper and magazine), outdoor (billboards, posters, banners, etc.), and digital (website, blogs, email, social media, etc.). Due to different size, space, cost, and attention of the readers; one standard written communication cannot be used for all the media for the purpose of marketing. More on this is discussed in the later section '*Writing online promotional content*'.

Specialised Writing

In addition to day-to-day formal communication containing instructions, requests, orders, information, memos, newsletter, etc.; the following are non-routine business communications, which require specific writing skills such as knowledge of law, technical language, written presentation skills, etc.

Drafting Agreements/Contracts

Writing or drafting matter involving agreement between parties needs extra care as the matter can involve legal issues. These agreements can be between employer and employees, supplier and manufacturer, sellers and buyers, between partners or associates, etc.

Examples of such agreements are appointment offer, service terms, partnership deed, price quote, supply contract, memorandum of understanding, guarantee/warranty terms, etc.

The writer needs to keep possible conflict and its solution in mind while drafting such agreements. Here, the objective of writing documents is not informing or persuading parties but to take their written agreement or binding on certain terms and conditions. Some documents are written with multiple complex sentences.

Reporting

The purpose of reporting is to describe the past events. Examples of events are financial results, achievements, updates, activities, incidents, etc. Reporting needs skills to narrate what happened or what was achieved. The writing must be based on fact, free from personal opinions, accurate, bias-free, and free from prejudice. Reporting includes informative tone rather than agreement or binding.

Manuals and SOP

Writing is also specific to manuals and Standard Operating Procedure (SOP). For example, manual for using equipment, manual to use laboratory, rule book, procedure for employees for appointment or transfer. Brevity and clarity are keys to write manuals and SOPs. Manuals and SOPs are developed in form of guidelines in form of 'how things work'. A set of steps for operations or procedures, mentioned in a numbered list, is the feature of this writing. Many times, manuals and SOPs include diagrams, symbols, signs, etc. also. This writing expects visualisation and problem-solving skills put on paper.

Digitized Communications

Written communications have changed from handwritten to typed (on typewriter) to computerised. SPAG (Spelling, Punctuations, and Grammar) is being taken care by the software. The younger generation is teaching the elder generation how to find and remember keys on keypads. Official communications are now-a-days not done via email only but also via texting (SMS) and instant messaging. Because of electronic mode of communications, the detailed written messages are becoming short and typed ones. Except for legal documents, certificates, etc. preference for soft copies has made the communication paperless.

Every employee is expected to be a computer literate. Though acquiring computer literacy takes time, it is worth to invest time looking at its advantages. The biggest advantage of digitized communication is that it saves a lot of time spent on editing while drafting the written communications. Thanks to the text/word processing software. Unlike in handwritten communication on papers, digitized communications do not compel communicators to tear off or discard drafts after drafts for the sake of correcting minute writing mistakes.

While transmitting digital communications there are incredibly useful features provided in email applications, as listed below:

1. flag the message according to priority to follow them up
2. search for a particular email in the inbox (by date, sender, or content of the message)
3. give high importance to emails
4. archive emails
5. move emails in folders
6. set vacation response
7. mark certain emails as spam/junk

Imagine how much time would be wasted if all of the above tasks are to be carried out for printed letters instead of email communications.

Digital mode of communications, especially emails, has given certain control to the sender in communication. Senders can access the read receipts so unlike in case of paper-based communications, receivers cannot lie about not receiving the message. The senders of emails can even recall the emails, which is impossible in case of sending messages via mail in hard copy. The similar control is available in case of communicating via instant messaging services too. It is significantly easier to keep track of messages received, sent, read, recalled, not delivered, and achieved. Due to digital modes, communications have become more transparent and systematic.

Writing Online Promotional Content

Every business needs to promote its products and its organisation. There are various ways to promote the business i.e., via TV, radio, newspapers, magazine, outdoor, and digital. Written content is not directly promoted on TV or radio while for the remaining platforms audience get exposed to the written promotional messages. Promotional content is to communicate to mass.

In last two decades, promotions of products on online media has become more popular among businesses. Though purpose of communication is the same (promotion), writing on online promotional platforms is different from writing for print media or for outdoor media. Comparatively, a large number of audience members can immediately react (likes, comments, share, etc.) to the communications written online. For example, promotional content published in print or outdoor media are not convenient for audience to react so quickly. The content on social media, emails, or on website receive immediate positive or negative reactions from the audience. While writing for online platforms, the writers should be aware that the message can get reactions from anyone irrespective of target audience for the message. For example, users of online platforms might give reactions even though they are not a stakeholder to the organisation posting the messages.

Online content should be written keeping probable reactions from mass, not just target audience. Now-a-days anyone can be offended for trivial reasons and in public spoil the image of the organisation making any message offensive.

There is a sea of content on online platforms including promotional content. While writing the content online, one should understand that in most of the cases, online readers ignore the clutter of promotional messages unless the messages create interest rather imposition. Promotional content writers should avoid excessive graphical elements such as product pictures, business event pictures, videos of award ceremonies, etc. These elements do not have much for the interest of audience. Online readers want brief and unfamiliar stories. Whether writers promote content for any social or political cause, marketable product, or fund raising for some charitable trust or for some social cause; the content should not try to sell anything rather should try to tell something. In the undercurrent of the told stories, the writer can weave the promotional message. Directly boasting about the business, its products, or organisation is not a good idea. Here follows the tips to plan and communicate on popular online promotional media:

Table 6

Tools/Platforms	*Tips*
Blogs	Write articles, not short posts. The articles should not be about the product or organisation directly but it must tell stories that lead readers to product or organisation.
Facebook/twitter posts	The content should be short and in the form of not only text but also image, video, animation, and other multimedia. Use hashtags.
Instagram stories/reels	The content must have impressive photographs and short videos. The content must not be longer than four swipes.
Quora answers	Must be longer than Facebook/Twitter posts but shorter than blog articles. More text and less multimedia. The answer must sound non promotional and informative. Must add reference links.
LinkedIn posts	The content should be for educated professional readers and formal not casual. Graphs and charts are used more than memes and caricatures.

For those who look after writing to promote the business, particularly on online platforms, must learn content marketing.

The tools/platforms mentioned in the table above are used to promote certain marketing content or messages. Content, such as articles, posts, stories, etc. are written for specific audience. The algorithm used by the platforms such as Facebook, Twitter, LinkedIn, Instagram, and Quora expose certain messages to certain audience based on age, preference, interest, location, etc. of the audience. So, the promotional content should be written for that particular audience and not for mass.

Writing is not gifted, it is a skill, which can be acquired. Written communications are recorded and can be retrieved unlike verbal communication. Written communications have their merits and challenges. There are certain accepted norms and expected standards followed while writing for business purposes. Specialised written business communications such as agreements, contracts, annual reports, compliance reports, marketing communications, etc. demand writers' training and experience. The written communications have become easier and more convenient to draft, transmit, and retrieve due to advent of word processing software, email applications, and the internet.

Notes

1. The act of beating someone or something with successive blows:the act of battering (https://www.merriam-webster.com/dictionary/battery#h1
2. Koerting Gayla, The myths behind President Abraham Lincoln as a speechwriter https://journalstar.com/news/opinion/the-myths-behind-president-abraham-lincoln-as-a-speechwriter/article_aae52d67-58de-5e21-8877-971642c195f2.html [accessed 22 Feb 2021]
3. John Wiley & Sons, Inc.. "The Secret Of Impressive Writing? Keep It Plain And Simple." ScienceDaily. ScienceDaily, 1 November 2005. <www.sciencedaily.com/releases/2005/10/051031075447.htm>.

Chapter - 8

Theory and Models in Communication

Theory and models in business literature helps us understand the phenomena and how are they generalised. Theory and models also explain the relationship among different variables in business communications. We can understand what happens, how it happens, and why it happens in business world though understanding theory and models. Theory and models also help us predict the pattern of communications.

Here follows the brief introduction of the widely used communication models and theory (presented in alphabetical order): An attempt has been made to describe theory and models related to interpersonal communication primarily and mass communication secondarily.

Models in communication

1. **AIDA Model:** AIDA stands for Attention – Interest – Desire – Action. In 1898, Elmo Lewis, one of the early advocates of methods in advertising and sales, develop this model to optimize sales calls.
2. **Aristotle Model of Communication:** 300 BCE, the Greek philosopher Aristotle developed and presented the model about communications. The model was about speakers, with other components such as speech, occasion, audience,

and effect. The model described one way communication from speakers to listeners.

Source: Authors' representation.

Figure 18: Components of Aristotle's Model of Communication.

Aristotle emphasised on speakers more than on speech, occasion, audience, or effect. Speaker, in this model, refer to the person qualities of the one who communicates. Speech refers to the content or the speaker's message. Occasion refers to the purpose of the speakers' communication. Audience means the receivers of the communication, and effect refers to the action or reaction of the speech.

3. **Barnlund model:** Barnlund model is also known as the transactional model of communication and it is believed to be the most systematic model on communications. The model was proposed in 1970 by Dean Barnlund. The major components of this model are person, decoding, encoding, public cues, private cues, and nonverbal behavioural cues. Filters, noise, experience, and simultaneous communications are other components presented in this model. Though the model is systematic, codes and complexity are the weaknesses of this model.
4. **Berlo's model:** In 1960, David Berlo presented the model, which is popular as SMCR model. SMCR stands for Sender, Message, Channel, and Receiver. This model is believed to be based on another model in communication developed by Shannon and Weaver. This was one of the earliest communication models discussing senders encoding the messages and receivers decoding the messages and effects. The subcomponents of SMCR are as shown in the table below:

Source	*Message*	*Channel*	*Receiver*
Communication skills	Elements	Seeing	Communication skills
Attitudes	Structure	Hearing	Attitudes
Knowledge	Content	Touching	Knowledge
Social system	Treatment	Smelling	Social system
Culture	Code	Tasting	Culture

5. **De Fleur Model of Communication:** This model is based on the one-way communication model by Shannon-weaver and the two-way communication model by Westley and Maclean. Mass media device, two-way feedback device, source, transmitter, receiver, and destination are the components of this model.
6. **Elaboration Likelihood Model (ELM):** In 1980, Richard Petty and John Cacioppo developed this model based on persuasion, stimuli processing, and attitudes.[1] The central and peripheral routes of persuasions described in this model are widely used in advertising and sales communications. The central route is associated with thinking while the peripheral is associated with cues. There are seven assumptions about variables and attitudes presented in this model. Motivation, ability, and determination are determinants of route.
7. **Fisher's Model:** Fisher's model was about group decision-making. In 1970, B. Aubrey Fisher gave an example of how ants communicate with one another. There were four phases Fisher proposed –(1) orientation, (2) conflict, (3) emergence, and (4) reinforcement.
8. **Gerbner's General Model:** Gerbner presented his general communication model in 1956. The two dimensions presented were perceptual dimension (with three factors i.e., selection, context, and availability) and means and controls dimension. The components of his model were event, man/machine, perceived message, signal/form, and content (by man/machine).

9. **Helical Model:** In 1967, Frank Dance proposed this model indicating the name of the model from helix. The model focused on problems in communications. Unlike many other models, Helical model is linear as well as circular. Dance suggested that communications do not perfectly repeat. People pass the received message with improvement, not as it is received. Communications grow from single and simple point to broader complex levels. The components of the model shows that communication is cyclical, influenced (by time and experience), continuous, nonrepetitive, and accumulative.
10. **Johari Window Model:** In 1955, psychologists Joseph Luft (Jo) and Harrington Ingham (Hari) developed this model. This model is used in corporate for team building and enhancing teamwork through improved communications among team members. Jo and Hari presented four quadrants (also known as 'selves') called open area, blind area, hidden area, and unknown area. To apply this model in real life, individuals are asked to describe themselves and others based on the words given. Knowledge, feelings, motivations, and information are components of this model. The model is used to check self-awareness and interpersonal relations.
11. **Lasswell's Model:** With a view to scientific study of communication process, Harold Lasswell developed this model in 1948. Lasswell defined communication as the answers to the questions –who says what, in which channel, to whom, with what effect?[2], referring to the components such as communicators, content, media, recipients, and outcome. In 1956, this model was expanded by George Gerbner focusing on perception and reaction.[3] Further, in 1958, Richard Braddock suggested that the model be expanded to consider two additional elements that Braddock argued it ignored: "for what purpose" and "under what circumstances".[4] McQuail and Windahl called this

model the most famous single phrase in communication research.[5]

12. **Newcomb's Model:** Theodore Newcomb introduced this model in 1953. It is also called the ABX model of communications, where A means sender, B means receiver, and X means matter of concern. The 'message' component is not included in his model, unlike many communication models.
13. **Osgood-Schramm Model:** Charles Osgood gave the idea of circular communication. Based on his circular communication model, Wilber Schramm developed the model in 1954. The major argument of this model is that communication is circular or two-directional, not linear. Rather than senders and receivers presented as different participants in other model, Osgood-Schramm model said they are the same party. Changing situation and feedback are in central components of this model along with encoder, message, decoder, and interpreter.
14. **Poole's Model:** Marshall Poole developed this model in 1983 focusing on group decision making processes. Three major components of Poole's model are developing strands, task accomplishment, and tracks of group activity.[6] This is also called the multiple sequence model. The variables or components discussed in this model are group composition, task structure, conflict management, task track, relation track, and topic track.
15. **Riley & Riley Model:** This model presented communicator and receiver individually connected to primary groups, which are parts of two larger social structures. Social structures are presented as the parts of overall social system. The difference between two primary groups in a social structure is the level of closeness in relationships with the group members. Group members can be friends, family members, relatives, or

colleagues. The basic concepts of the model are two-way communications, interdependent and interrelated feedback, and social context.

16. **Shannon–Weaver Model:** While working with Bell Telephone Labs, Claude Shannon and Warren Weaver expanded Shannon's *a mathematical theory of communication* and developed a communication model in 1949. The model is a one-way communication and explained the role of noise in the communication process. Components of Shannon-Weaver model are information source, transmitter, channel, receiver, and destination.
17. **Westley and Maclean Model:** Proposed in 1957, Westley and Maclean model is a two-way communication and for first time they introduced the important component called "Linear Feedback" in the communication model. The model is based on Newcomb's ABX model of communication. The authors Bruce Westley and Malcolm S. MacLean Jr. argued that the communication is not just the initiation from the senders. Communication is not completed until the receivers respond. In addition to interpersonal communication, the model is applicable to mass communication also. The components of this model are source, message, interpretation, receiver, feedback, environment, sensory experience, objects of orientation, receiver, object of orientation of receiver, gatekeeper, opinion leader.

Theory in Communication

1. **A Mathematical Theory of Communication:** In 1948, C. E. Shannon published an article "A Mathematical Theory of Communication" in the Bell System Technical Journal[7]. In 1949, Warren Weaver added an article to this theory and their work was published in a book form. Shannon's theory gave birth to the modern information

theory. The idea of the theory was the isolation of communication signals from the meaning of the message communicated. Magnitude of the communicated message is not directly related with the magnitude of message conveyed by a signal.

2. **Accommodation Theory:** Communication Accommodation Theory state that while communicating, people accommodate or adjust one another understanding others' background. The components of this theory are the sociohistorical context, the communicators' accommodative orientation, the immediate situation, and evaluation and future intentions. This theory applies to intergroup and interpersonal communications and says that thoughts and ideas are invented. This invention happens through culture in societies.
3. **Functional Group Communication Theory:** Dennis Gouran and Randy Hirokawa proposed this theory in 1983[8]. The major focus of the functional group communication theory is the decision quality in a balanced group decision making process. It is also known as functional theory of communication. Four components or functions of group decision are problem analysis, goal setting, identity alternatives, and evaluate and select. The theory says that communication plays three roles: a promotive role, a disruptive role, and a counteractive role. This theory is influenced by John Dewey's thinking and problem solving, Robert Bales's four functional problems, and Irving Janis's Groupthink.
4. **Genderlect Theory:** This theory is based on the idea that men and women communicate or use the communication not for the same purpose or with the same communication ritual. Deborah Tannen coined the term *Genderlect* in her book *You Just Don't Understand: Women and Men in Conversations* in 1990.

5. **Groupthink Theory:** This theory state that people try to have consensus within a group and for the sake of agreement or conformity within a group, the group members make negative or positive decisions. Irving Janis introduced this term and the theory in 1972. The symptoms of Groupthink are illusion of invulnerability, belief in inherent morality of the group, collective rationalisation, out-group stereotypes, self-censorship, illusion of unanimity, direct pressure on dissenters, and self-appointed mind-guards.
6. **Muted Group Theory:** Edwin Ardener and Shirley Ardener developed the muted group theory in 1975. The idea of this theory is that the language is used to mute the marginalised group. The components of this theory are dominant group, dominant language, language system, social norms, subordinate group, mutedness, perception of reality, ridicule, ritual, control, harassment, etc.
7. **Narrative Paradigm Theory:** Walter Fisher developed narrative paradigm theory. In 1987, Fisher introduced two universal paradigms – the rational world paradigm, and the narrative paradigm[9]. The idea of the narrative paradigm theory was that storytelling or reporting form of communication is more convincing and explaining the complex information. This paradigm was proposed to be used for dealing with *public moral argument issues.*
8. **Social Exchange Theory:** The idea proposed by George Homans in this theory is that exchange process causes social behaviour with the objectives of minimizing risks or costs and maximizing behaviour.[10] By comparing benefits with costs, people decide whether the relationship or exchange is positive or negative. The major component of Homans's theory are equilibration, expectancy, distributive justice, dyadic exchange, success, stimulus, and deprivation– satiation. Other researchers who contributed

to the theory were Peter Blau, Richard Emerson, John Thibaut, Harold Kelley, Claude Lévi-Strauss, etc.

9. **Social Learning Theory:** In 1963 and further in 1977, Albert Bandura described the factors affecting human behaviour and learning. According to this theory, environmental factors and cognitive factors are influencers on the behaviour and learning. Behaviour is acquired through imitation and observation. The major components described in this theory are learning, observation, cognitive, vicarious reinforcement, attention, retention, reproduction, motivation, etc.

10. **Social Penetration Theory:** Irwin Altman and Dalmas Taylor developed this theory in 1973 as a part of studying how relationships between individuals are developed. The four basic assumptions of this theory are– (1) from superficial layers, relationship development transits to intimate layers. (2) relationships are developed in systematic way. (3) the development can move backward towards dissolution, and (4) relationship development can be facilitated by self-disclosure.

Chronology of Popular Models and Theory in Communication

Year	*Model/theory*	*Proposed by*	*Major components*
300 BCE	Aristotle Model of Communication	Aristotle	speech, occasion, audience, and effect
1898	AIDA Model	Elmo Lewis	Attention, interest, desire, and action
1948	Lasswell's model	Harold Lasswell	communicators, content, media, recipients, and outcome
1949	A mathematical theory of communication	C. E. Shannon	Signals, meaning, magnitude, information theory
1949	Shannon–Weaver Model	Claude Shannon and Warren Weaver	information source, transmitter, channel, receiver, and destination
1953	Newcomb's Model/ ABX model	Theodore Newcomb	sender, receiver, and matter of concern
1954	Osgood-Schramm Model	Charles Osgood and Wilber Schramm	Changing situation, feedback, encoder, message, decoder, and interpreter

(*Cond...*)

1955	JoHari Window Model	Joseph Luft & Harrington Ingham	Knowledge, feelings, motivations, and information
1956	Gerbner's general communication model	Gerbner	event, man/machine, perceived message, signal/form, and content (by man/machine)
1957	Westley and Maclean Model	Bruce Westley and Malcolm S. MacLean Jr.	Linear feedback, source, message, interpretation, receiver, environment, sensory experience, objects of orientation, receiver, gatekeeper, and opinion leader
1958	Social Exchange Theory	George Homans	equilibration, expectancy, distributive justice, dyadic exchange, success, stimulus, and deprivation–satiation
1959	Riley & Riley Model	John W. Riley and Matilda White Riley	two-way communications, interdependent and interrelated feedback, and social context
1960	Berlo's SMCR model	David Berlo	Communication skills, elements, seeing, attitude, structure, hearing, knowledge, content, touching, social system, treatment, smelling, culture, code, tasting
1963	Social Learning Theory	Albert Bandura	learning, observation, cognitive, vicarious reinforcement, attention, retention, reproduction, and motivation
1967	Helical model	Frank Dance	cyclical, influenced (by time and experience), continuous, nonrepetitive, and accumulative communication
1970	Barnlund model/transactional model	Dean Barnlund	person, decoding, encoding, public cues, private cues, and nonverbal behavioural cues
1970	Fisher's Model	B. Aubrey Fisher	orientation, conflict, emergence, and reinforcement.
1972	Groupthink theory	Irving Janis	illusion of invulnerability, belief in inherent morality of the group, collective rationalization, out-group stereotypes, self-censorship, illusion of unanimity, direct pressure on dissenters, and self-appointed mindguards

(*Cond...*)

1973	Social Penetration Theory	Irwin Altman & Dalmas Taylor	Development, superficial layers, intimate layers, self-disclosure
1975	Muted Group Theory	Edwin Ardener & Shirley Ardener	are dominant group, dominant language, language system, social norms, subordinate group, mutedness, perception of reality, ridicule, ritual, control, and harassment
1970s-80s	De Fleur's various models	Melvin Lawrence De Fleur	Mass media device, two-way feedback device, source, transmitter, receiver, and destination
1980	Elaboration Likelihood Model (ELM)	Richard Petty and John Cacioppo	central and peripheral routes of persuasions
1983	Poole's Model	Marshall Poole	group composition, task structure, conflict management, task track, relation track, and topic track
1983	Functional Group Communication Theory	Dennis Gouran and Randy Hirokawa	problem analysis, goal setting, identity alternatives, and evaluate and select
1987	Narrative Paradigm Theory	Walter Fisher	rational world paradigm, and narrative paradigm
1990	Genderlect theory	Deborah Tannen	Gender, purpose, ritual
1991	Accommodation Theory	Giles, Coupland, & Coupland	sociohistorical context, communicators' accommodative orientation, immediate situation, evaluation, and future intentions

Notes

1. Petty, Richard; Cacioppo, John (1986). The elaboration likelihood model of persuasion. *Advances in Experimental Social Psychology*. London, England: Elsevier. 19: 124 129. doi:10.1016/s0065-2601(08)60214-2. ISBN 9780120152193.
2. Lasswell, Harold (1948). Bryson, L. (ed.). The Structure and Function of Communication in Society. *The Communication of Ideas*. New York: Institute for Religious and Social Studies. p. 117.
3. Berger, A. (1995). Essentials of Mass Communication Theory. Thousand Oaks: Sage Publications. p. 14.
4. Braddock, Richard (1958). "An Extension of the "Lasswell Formula"". *Journal of Communication. 8: 88–93. doi:10.1111/j.1460-2466.1958.tb01138.x.*

5. McQuail, Denis; Windahl, Sven (1993). Communication models for the study of mass communications (2nd ed.). New York: Longman. pp. 13–15.
6. Poole, Marshall Scott (1983-12-01). "Decision development in small groups, III: A multiple sequence model of group decision development". *Communication Monographs*. 50 (4): 321–341. doi:10.1080/03637758309390173. ISSN 0363-7751.
7. Shannon, Claude Elwood (July 1948). "A Mathematical Theory of Communication" (PDF). *Bell System Technical Journal*, 27 (3): 379–423. doi:10.1002/j.1538-7305.1948.tb01338.x. hdl:11858/00-001M-0000-002C-4314-2.http://people.math.harvard.edu/~ctm/home/text/others/shannon/entropy/entropy.pdf [Accessed 21 Mar 2021]
8. Gouran, D. S., & Hirokawa, R. Y. (1983). The role of communication in decision-making groups: A functional perspective. In M. S. Mander (Ed.), *Communications in transition* (pp. 168–185). New York: Praeger.
9. Fisher, Walter R. (1987). Human Communication as Narration: Toward a Philosophy of Reason, Value, and Action. Columbia: University of South Carolina Press.
10. Homans, George (1961). Social Behavior: Its Elementary Forms. New York: Harcourt Brace Jovanovich. p. 13.

Index

D

E

F

G

H

I

P